LIGHT

on the

HEAVY

**A simple guide
to understanding
Bible doctrines.**

by Jerry Jenkins

This book is designed for your personal reading
pleasure and profit. It is also designed for group
study. A leader's guide, with visual aids
(SonPower Multiuse Transparency Masters) is
available from your local Christian bookstore or
from the publisher.

VICTOR BOOKS

a division of SP Publications, Inc., Wheaton, Illinois
Offices also in Fullerton, California • Whitby, Ontario, Canada • London, England

Second printing, 1978

Library of Congress Catalog Card Number: 78-056613
ISBN: 0-88207-769-4

VICTOR BOOKS
A Division of SP Publications, Inc.
P.O. Box 1825 • Wheaton, Ill. 60187

areas of that teaching is known individually as *a* Bible doctrine. Bible doctrines are facts. Believe them or not, they're still facts. They're not people's opinions; they're what God Himself actually teaches: the truth. And the truth—pleasant or unpleasant—is what you want if you're a true disciple of Christ.

Nobody's summary of Bible doctrine is perfect though. In this process of summarizing so much truth briefly, even the most careful scholars may misinterpret Scripture, reflecting their biases, maybe even omitting something important. You might even run across two explanations of "Bible doctrine" that contradict each other at certain points. Obviously one—or both—is in error. All creeds and summary statements—including the ones in the book you're reading right now—need to be checked with the Bible itself. Not just with an apparent "proof text" or two, but with all that the Bible says on a given subject. That's not always easy, but it's worth the trouble. A Bible doctrine *overview* (which this book is) can get you started.

The most important ideas aren't all that hard to get a handle on. They're definite. Christians may hold different opinions about minor details of interpretations or application, but the basic doctrines of the Bible are so clear that all who study them agree on their essential meanings.

You have a good head start in this study (and in the Christian life) if you've attended Sunday School and Bible preaching services for a few years—especially if you've also done a little thoughtful Bible reading on your own. Everything you already know about God and His truth is doctrine whether you've ever called it that or not. But when you dig further you'll find there's more to each doctrine than you ever dreamed.

It's the stuff to live by if you want the maximum joy in life. But that's stating it backward. Your joy, according to Jesus' teaching, will come as a by-product when you first seek God's joy and others'. (For Scripture on that point, try Matthew 6:33-34; 16:25; Romans 12:1-12; 14:8; 15:2-7; and Philippians 2:3-11.)

No one can see the whole picture of his life the way God does. No one can understand all that God tells him. But our seeing and our understanding can expand. Some of it already makes sense if you know Christ. In a nutshell, God the Creator has provided for our very greatest need by allowing His Son, Jesus, to suffer death for our sin. God's guarantee is the fact that He then raised Jesus from death, to be our Saviour and Lord forever. He has also given His Holy Spirit to be our divine Companion on earth till He receives us into the unimaginably exciting eternal future with Him.

Just before Jesus ascended to heaven, He told His disciples to teach everybody *all* that He'd commanded (Matthew 28:18-20). Why did He make such a big point about everybody, including you, learning *all* that He'd commanded? He wants to be not just your Saviour but also your life! He wants you to have purpose and joy—gifts that can be yours only when you're His learning, growing disciple.

That's what makes Bible doctrine beautiful. It's lively stuff for live Christians. And it gives you not just a head start but also a heart start.

Love plus

I once taught a Sunday School class of junior high boys. The lesson manual encouraged the teacher to emphasize to the class members that Jesus loves them individually. At one point the manual suggested that the teacher ask all the students to say *Jesus loves me* to themselves whenever that thought hit them during the week. *Hmm,* I thought, *that's interesting. I'll try it. I'll tell the boys not to think of it in terms of the song we'd all learned as little kids, nor just in the general sense that Jesus loves everyone, but to realize that it's as true for each kid alone, as if he were the ONLY one Jesus loves.*

When class time came, I was ready. Being only ten years older than the boys. I remembered all too well the frustrations of junior highers. And now I'd studied this lesson and was all psyched up with concern for each boy. But somehow when I got to the "Jesus loves me" part of the lesson, it didn't work quite as I'd planned. I went through the lines the way they appeared in the manual, but as I concluded the lesson, the truth of it all hit *me* between the eyes.

I was telling the kids, "Don't use the words simply as a cheap psychological trick to make yourself feel better. Realize that it's true, just for you. 'Jesus loves *me!* Jesus loves *me!*' " But as I talked to them the thought affected me so deeply that I could hardly get the words out. While encouraging others to make personal that simple yet profound truth, I felt all over again how much Jesus loves *me*. The experience was overpowering.

The God of the universe—infinite, unimaginable, unfathomable—loves you and me. Not just when we're fired up emotionally or on a spiritual high, but now, then, tomorrow, always. He loves us whether we respond to His love or not. That's why His Word and His Spirit and His Church all plead with people to respond to His Gospel rather than to remain alienated from Him and deprived of what He can do for them in this life and the next. He loves us even when we go our stubborn ways in disobedience to Him. That's why His Word and His Spirit and His Church send out warnings of the judgment which will come to those who refuse His grace. So you see, even the short phrase "Jesus loves me" can be heavy doctrine.

There's much more to doctrine, of course. And, yes, a lot of it is heavy—deep and complex. But each part of the truth we call Bible doctrine can be as beautiful, light, and moving to you as that simple children's song was to me that day with my junior high boys.

Facts plus

As you study the following chapters, I want you to discover above all that Bible doctrine is more than facts to tuck into the back of your head. As Dr. Francis Patton says in a book called *A Summary of Christian Doctrine* (Westminister Press), "The doctrines claim a position above all other truth because of their *practical value*." This kind of truth belongs in our day-to-day thoughts and actions. It will motivate us to be and do our best as people who know God. And it will focus on the One who'll give us the *ability* to be and do our best for His honor, for others' benefit, and for our own satisfaction. Open-minded, open-hearted study of Bible doctrine is the key.

If you've thought that doctrine is dull, maybe it's because it is often packaged in dry outline form, seemingly written as far away from life as possible. Some outlines simply give you abstract statements of theology, soteriology, eschatology, and other such unfamiliar "ologies." The "ologies" are all relevant—but their relevance isn't always clear. Let's look at each "ology" from where you are. We'll start with the doctrine of you (the doctrine of man), and as we move on to the other doctrines, we'll keep relating them to you and your life. And we'll see that the answers to such big questions as who am I, why am I here, and where am I going, are in the Bible.

We'll also take note of God's fairness and man's unfairness. God's sin*less*ness and man's sin*ful*-ness create a huge problem, as you know. It calls for drastic action. That brings us to the special roles of Jesus Christ and the Holy Spirit, along with the role of the heavenly Father.

God's chief enemy, who is also *our* chief enemy, will get a closer look too. And then we'll move on to the doctrines of salvation, and of the church, and of angels, (still doing great things on earth), and of events yet future.

This may sound out of touch with your life, but I think you'll discover that it's actually more *in* touch with you than anything else. God's truth, all of it, applies to your life and to the lives of your family, your friends, everyone else you know, including your enemies. And as someone said, "To the Christian, nothing is secular except what is sinful."

This book is designed to help you see how Bible doctrine fits your life. Let it!

Sandwiched in with each chapter of this book you'll find a list of words, headed "Unbind Your Mind." Each word is accompanied by a short definition that explains what the word means as it's used in this book or in Scripture. Don't memorize these definitions. But refer to them if you come to a word whose meaning you're not sure of.

Not Really a Riddle
but it'll make you think

1. Not all religious doctrine is the truth of God (Ephesians 4:14). Check out Mark 7:6-8 to see what Jesus said about the value of any worship based on doctrines that are man-made rather than God-made.

2. Do you sometimes wonder how to be sure certain religious teachings are really the truth of God? Jesus' words in John 7:17 give you a special clue. Read that verse in as many versions as you can. Then write a paragraph that explains the difference between mere curiosity and a sincere desire to know and live by God's truth.

Unbind Your Mind
with these capsule definitions

creed—a short formal statement of doctrinal belief, sometimes called a confession of faith or an affirmation of faith

disciple—a faithful follower; a trusting, obedient learner

doctrine—teaching (usally this word refers to the content of teaching)

holy—perfect; separated to God and from sin

sacred—dedicated to God or belonging to Him

secular—not dedicated to God and not belonging to Him

theology—the study of God and what He reveals

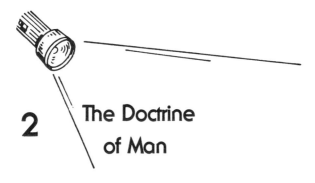

2 The Doctrine of Man

All the doctrines of the Bible deal with man in one way or another, for the Bible is God's message, His Word *to us*. And one proof of the Bible's divine authorship is that it meets so exactly the needs of our hearts and minds, in ways that only our Creator could know.

Scientists call their study of man *anthropology*. So do theologians. So what does the Bible say about man?

For our study of this doctrine (and for most of the other doctrines too), let's take a simple, direct approach, using these three questions: What does the Bible say? What does it mean? How does it apply to you?

What the Bible says about man
The first thing the Bible says about man is that we were created in the image of God. "And God created man in His own image, in the image of God He created him; male and female He created them" (Genesis 1:27).

Another basic teaching is that man was given authority over the earth. "God blessed them; and God said to them, 'Be fruitful and multiply, and fill the earth, and subdue it; and rule over the fish of the sea and over the birds of the sky, and over every living thing that moves on the earth'" (Genesis 1:28).

The Bible also clearly teaches that the first man and woman were created perfect and sinless. We all know the story of the forbidden fruit, Satan tempting Eve, and the willful choice both Eve and Adam made to commit the first human sin—the act of disobedience which ended both their personal innocence and the innocence of the human race. Their sin, as you know, resulted in the death sentence for themselves and for all their descendants. For the whole story, read Genesis 3 and Romans 5:12-19.

What It means

The Genesis record shows us immediately that we are valuable to God. Man was God's final creation, but he was first in God's mind. Everything God made was good, but He did something extra special when He made man. Man is God's masterpiece.

The story of man's creation is told in Genesis 1—2. The second chapter gives the most details.

After forming man "of dust from the ground," God "breathed into his nostrils the breath of life" (Genesis 2:7). That breath of life made man a unique living being.

Most of your body is water, a combination of oxygen and hydrogen—elements that are found in the earth's soil as well as in the air. Your body also contains carbon, iron, calcium, chlorine, and other earthy elements. But your coming from the earth (via your parents and ancestors) does not fully explain your life. The "breath of God" made Adam—and all his descendants—creatures of unique worth to God.

The value God places on all people shows up in this 3,000-year-old poem by David:

"What is man, that Thou dost take thought of him? ... Thou hast made him a little lower than God, and dost crown him with glory and majesty!"

(Psalm 8:4-5)

Man has a *soul*. The soul is something that no biologist can dissect or explain, though recently some leading scientists have become fascinated by the subject and are seeking for man's soul through psychological research.

Man, created in God's image, is not like God in physical appearance, but in his possession of personhood. The Apostle Paul referred to man's unique nature when he wrote to a group of Christians: "May your *spirit and soul and body* be preserved complete" (1 Thessalonians 5:23).

Being in God's image gives us marvelous abilities. We have minds, emotions, wills, and consciences. These four powers are what make us completely different from animals:

You can think. With paper and pencil you can plan the route of a camping trip, work out menus, figure the cost of the food, do your schoolwork. And God has not only given you the ability to exercise logic but He also invites you to *think with Him.* " 'Come now, and let us reason together,' says the Lord" (Isaiah 1:18).

You can feel emotion. Emotions add color to your life—whether it's excitement about a basket-

ball victory, happiness about a friend's being reunited with her parents, or sadness when your
uncle dies. Feelings can serve God as we learn to
share the feelings of others. "Rejoice with those
who rejoice, and weep with those who weep"
(Romans 12:15).

You can choose. You can tell your friends, "I
will" or "I won't." You can decide to obey your
parents or you can decide not to. God lets you
make spiritual choices too. "I have set before you
life and death, the blessing and the curse. So
choose life" (Deuteronomy 30:19).

*You can know right from wrong with your con-
science.* God, whose sense of right and wrong is
perfect and absolute, expects you to train your
conscience by studying His Word and honestly
making right choices. If you lie or are tempted to
lie, a conscience tuned to God makes you uneasy.
As Christians we are to "maintain always a
blameless conscience both before God and before men" (Acts 24:16).

We have these unique abilities for a purpose.
In answer to the question, "What is the chief
end (purpose) of man?" an old saying replies,
"The chief end of man is to glorify God and
enjoy Him forever." Many different Scripture
passages confirm that idea.

In His original instructions to Adam, God gave
him the authority and responsibility to take care
of plant life as well as animal life; and God gave
him the right to use these things for food and
shelter. As God's steward, man is expected to
think, plan and properly manage the land, air,
water, and living things about him. Such
authority/responsibility extends to his relation-

ships with other people, as we can see in the Ten Commandments and other Scripture passages.

Throughout the centuries, man has achieved much when he has properly exercised his authority over nature. By cultivating and harvesting fields and orchards, harnessing oxen and horses, fishing, milking cows and goats, recycling wastes, building dams, he has fulfilled part of his potential as the God-appointed manager of the earth. But he has often acted unwisely: wasting whole forests by cutting without replanting; polluting the air with smoke and auto exhaust; poisoning the water with the vile wastes from factories; overconsuming natural resources; and producing hazardous radioactivity by nuclear manufacturing. Worse yet, people mistreat other people by cheating, lying, stealing, and killing, both as individuals and as nations. And worst of all, people rebel against God who created them and loves them.

Man was not always sinful. Adam and Eve were created perfect, sinless. And God entrusted them with power to choose. They'd been warned clearly: "From any tree of the garden you may eat freely; but from the tree of the knowledge of good and evil you shall not eat, for in the day that you eat from it you shall surely die" (Genesis 2:16-17). That didn't seem unfair till Satan came around, first questioning God's statement and then contradicting it. Then they both committed the sin of disobedience—rebelling against their Creator.

When they ate the forbidden fruit, they immediately became spiritually dead, and were doomed to die physically. Through that introduction of sin into the human family, the same fate came upon all mankind.

Since the time of Adam and Eve, everyone has been born with the fatal disease of sin permeating his very being. Paul wrote: "Through one man sin entered into the world, and death through sin, and so death spread to all men, because all sinned" (Romans 5:12). How important it is, then, for all of us sinners to know the one Saviour from sin. "For as in Adam all die, so also in Christ all shall be made alive" (1 Corinthians 15:22). Salvation (life instead of death) comes by God's grace through faith in Jesus Christ.

Apart from Christ we can do nothing to heal our disease of sinfulness. An Old Testament prophet put it this way: "All of us have become like one who is unclean, and all our righteous deeds are like a filthy garment; and all of us wither like a leaf, and our iniquities, like the wind, take us away" (Isaiah 64:6). Total depravity does not mean that we are totally evil. It means rather that every part of us is infected with evil— our minds, our emotions, our wills, our consciences, our motivations, even our bodies.

Yet our entire beings can be redeemed. Through repentance and faith in the One who came to redeem sinners, we can regain our freedom, our ability to serve God acceptably, and our capacity to enjoy God.

How does all this apply to you?

You, like everyone else, were created *in the image of God.*

You, with them, share authority and responsibility for what happens in this world.

And you too were born with the fatal disease of sin. You see the symptoms every day.

Think awhile about being in the image of God. Doesn't that realization do something great for your *self*-image? You, personally, like God Himself, have powers of mind, emotion, will, and conscience which you can use every day. God loves you—even respects you—because you are in His image! And even though sin has affected your God-like abilities, a maturing relationship with Jesus Christ can increasingly bring out the best in you. If you keep Him at the center of your life, you'll become a vibrant and happy person.

Think again about being in the image of God—this time about your best friend being in God's image. Does that add a whole new dimension to your friendship? Apply the same thought seriously to your *least-favorite* person. Does it begin to stimulate a Christlike attitude toward him or her? It can help you start relating to that person in a more positive way.

Now think awhile about your God-given authority and responsibility for things in this world. Maybe you can't stop air pollution, or fix the San Andreas fault, or command the U.S. Department of Agriculture to have farmers raise a billion tons of grain for the world's starving peoples. But there are some things you can do right where you are to help preserve our natural resources and put them to their proper uses.

Now think about your being a sinner, by nature and by action. If you've already turned to Christ for salvation, you've already received full pardon. You can get help from God every day for whatever temptations you face, and you can receive renewed cleansing as you need it. But if you don't yet know Christ as your Saviour, then your sin and guilt is your worst problem, whether you realize it or not. Why the worst? Because it's separating you from God.

Remember, though, that God *loves* sinners (John 3:16-17); Christ *died to save* sinners (Matthew 1:21; 1 Timothy 1:15); and by receiving His free gift of salvation you can be among those whose sins are completely forgiven by God (Psalms 32:1-5; 86:5; 103:11-12; 1 John 1:8-9).

Lots of *why* questions must be left for discussions in heaven. Meanwhile, there's a lot for us to know about *who* (you!) and *when* (right now and forever!) and *how* (by a living-faith relationship to God).

Exercises for Your Brains, Hands and Hearts

Brain: Adam and Eve became sinners by sinning, rebelling against God's authority. How about all their offspring? Do we become sinners by sinning, or do we sin because we're sinners? Base your answer on at least two of the Scripture passages listed in this chapter.

Hands: Think of a specific way you can help care for God's earth this week. Do it.

Heart: Read Psalm 139, a prayer poem. After you get the feel of how David personally sensed his intimate relationship with God, write a short prayer of your own on the same theme.

Unbind Your Mind
with these capsule definitions

anthropology—the study of man

finite—limited in time, space, and power

image of God—likeness of God (God created man in His likeness, giving him a spiritual nature with intellect, emotions, power of choice, and potential for fellowship with God)

infinite—unlimited in time, space, and power

man or mankind—human beings, created with souls and spirits as well as bodies.

soul—a person's undying, non-material *self*; the real you inside

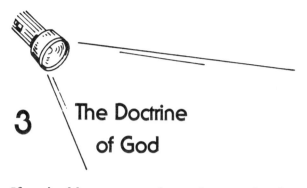

3

The Doctrine
of God

If you're like most people, you've wondered, at one time or another, where God came from. How He began. Why He exists. And now, at last, you've found this book!

Well, I'm sorry to disappoint you but you won't find the answers in this or any other book. Not even in the Bible. A lot of things about God are way beyond us.

Sometimes I've tried to picture myself in heaven. I've wondered what I'll do there, what it will look like, what it will feel like. And I've tried to imagine living there *forever*. Not just the *long, long time* kind of forever, but *forever* forever. Well, it's not too hard to imagine *beginning* my life in heaven (either when I die or when Jesus returns). But when I try to imagine *eternity*, my mind nearly shorts out.

If that thought doesn't boggle your mind, try imagining God's eternal existence. The "age" of God goes back long before the creation of anything. Now go back father than that in your imagination ... farther ... you could never go back far enough. Why? Because God never began. He has always existed. One of God's characteristics is that He is really eternal—without end, without beginning!

God's eternal existence is just one of the many attributes that characterize the one and only God and Creator of the universe. His other attributes are also hard to understand, but they mean much to us because of the way they touch our lives.

What the Bible says about God

The following verses verify the eternality of God. "Before the mountains were born, or Thou didst give birth to the earth and the world, even from everlasting to everlasting, Thou art God" (Psalm 90:2). " 'I am the Alpha and the Omega,' says the Lord God, 'who is and who was and who is to come, the Almighty' " (Revelation 1:8).

In a Moody Correspondence School course called "The Bible Says," Dr. James M. Gray shows from many different passages that God is *infinite*—totally unlimited in His power and scope. He is greater than time; greater than space; greater by far than anything and everything He has made. "Great is our Lord and abundant in strength; His understanding is infinite" (Psalm 147:5). Because language is limited, even with a 50,000-word vocabulary, the Bible writers often simply exclaimed, "*Great* is the Lord, and greatly to be praised!" (Psalm 48:1)

Besides His eternal and infinite nature, theologians also talk a lot about God's *moral* attributes:

• Truth—God cannot lie (Titus 1:2).

• Justice—"He will do no injustice. Every morning He brings His justice to light. He does not fail" (Zephaniah 3:5).

• Love—"God is love" (1 John 4:8).

• Goodness—"Thou art good and doest good" (Psalm 119:68). "There is only One who is good" (Matthew 19:17).

• Holiness—Moses sang about God's holiness (Exodus 15:11); God Himself said that He is holy (Leviticus 20:26); the supernatural seraphim in Isaiah's vision called out the fact that God is holy (Isaiah 6:3); and in his vision of heaven the Apostle John saw and heard God's holiness being sung about in a still-future super-singspiration (Revelation 15:4).

The very basic doctrine about God is of course that there is *only one* God. God Himself emphasized that fact when He gave the Law to Moses. "Know therefore today, and take it to your heart, that the Lord, He is God in heaven above and on the earth below; there is no other" (Deuteronomy 4:39). The Apostle Paul emphasized this same truth when he wrote: "one God and Father of all who is over all and through all and in all" (Ephesians 4:6).

Yet the one God exists as three Persons— Father, Son, and Spirit—the Trinity. All three Persons are clearly identified as God in the Bible, yet They are distinct. In fact, sometimes all three are mentioned in a single sentence of Scripture. For example, in 2 Corinthians 13:14 Paul gives this greeting: "The grace of the Lord Jesus Christ, and the love of God, and the fellowship of the Holy Spirit be with you all."

Another wonderful thing about God is that He never changes. For imperfect beings such as ourselves, change is often necessary and can be very good. But for God, who is perfect, change is never necessary. He always remains true to Himself. God is "the Father of lights, with whom there is no variation, or shifting shadow" (James 1:17).

What's the meaning?

You can represent three aspects of God's unlimited nature by the three "O's" that you've probably heard about in Sunday school or in sermons: God is *omniscient, omnipresent* and *omnipotent.*

What does "omniscient" mean? "Omni" means *all,* and "scient" (as in "science") means *knowing.* When we say God is omniscient we mean He is all-knowing. God knows what is happening *all over the globe* and beyond, not just what is happening in one place He knows everything that has happened and everything yet to happen! He knows not only what happens but exactly how it happens and why. And He knows each individual personally, and this includes all our innermost thoughts and attitudes. No wonder Paul exclaimed, "Oh, the depth of the riches both of the wisdom and knowledge of God!" (Romans 11:33)

What does "God is omnipresent" mean? In this word, "omni" teams up with the word "present" to describe God as being everywhere all the time. This is possible because He is the unlimited Spirit, never locked in by time or space. Right now He is millions of light years away, out among the distant galaxies, and at the same moment He is right there with you. God says, "Can a man hide himself in hiding places, so I do not see him? . . . Do I not fill the heavens and the earth?" (Jeremiah 23:24)

What does "God is omnipotent" mean? It

means that He is *all-powerful*. The God who created the universe and everything in it can do anything He wants to do. In the first book of the Bible, He says of Himself: "I am God Almighty" (Genesis 17:1). The Prophet Jeremiah's response to the thought of God's power is summed up in this exclamation: "Ah, Lord God! Behold, Thou hast made the heavens and the earth by Thy great power and by Thine outstretched arm! Nothing is too difficult for Thee" (Jeremiah 32:17). Some people like to ask questions such as: Can God create a rock too heavy for Him to lift? Such absurdities mean nothing because they are inconsistent with God's purpose and nature. God uses His power only to further His kingdom and to perform acts of justice, love, and mercy toward His people.

God's moral attributes are all consistent with each other even though they may not seem to be at first glance. Take, for example, God's holiness and His love. He is completely holy (sinless and intolerant of sin). Yet He loves all sinners completely.

Something that's impossible for our finite minds to grasp is the mystery of the Trinity—the "three Gods in one Being." "There is no God but One." That's a direct quote from 1 Corinthians 8:4. But isn't Jesus God? And what about the Holy Spirit? Isn't He God too?

Jesus distinctly said that there is only one God: "Hear, O Israel: The Lord our God is one Lord; and you shall love the Lord your God with all your heart, and with all your soul, and with all your mind, and with all your strength" (Mark 12:29-30). Yet Jesus also said, "I and the Father are one" (John 10:30). The one God shows Himself to us as three Persons united in one Being.

The truth that there is only one God is called His *unity*, while the truth that He is three Persons is called His *tri-unity* or trinity. Some things about the infinite God can be expected to be beyond the comprehension of finite humans. The Trinity is one such mystery.

Some people have tried to illustrate the concept of the Trinity by pointing out that H_2O is H_2O, not just when it's liquid, but also when it's frozen and when it's steam. Similarly, they say, God is God whether He appears as Father, Son, or Holy Spirit. But this illustration falls far short because in the Trinity each Person is truly separate. At times all Three are present at once (as at Jesus' baptism or when you pray). Perhaps this diagram will help clarify the meaning of the Trinity for you, though it can't explain *how* it can be.

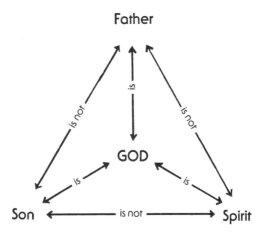

The fact that God never changes doesn't mean that He never changes His course of action or His method of dealing with people. Sometimes He has withdrawn judgment that He had been ready to release on rebellious people. Remember Nineveh after Jonah's warning? God often makes adjustments in His dealings with us too, but always His actions are consistent with His unchanging character. He withdrew judgment from Nineveh, for example, because the people repented. To inflict punishment on them after they had turned to Him in repentance would have been inconsistent with His love and justice. Perhaps a better word for this attribute of God is *faithfulness.* God never goes back on His promises. You can count on everything He says. He always remains true to His own character of justice, love, goodness, and holiness.

How does all this apply to you?

Knowing. There's so much that you and I cannot understand about God—His infinity, His eternality, His omniscience, His omnipresence, His omnipotence, His tri-unity, His holiness, His justice, His unconditional love. Yet you can know Him well enough to come to Him for release from your sins through the Lord Jesus Christ. Just as you can benefit from electricity without understanding it, so you can benefit from God's power without understanding it. But God does expect you to increase your knowledge of Him through studying and obeying His Word—learning by doing.

Trusting. If you're a Christian, you are already plugged into the ultimate Power Source. And God has never had a power failure. But your vital connection with God is faith *in* Him, not just knowledge about Him. "Without faith it is impossible to please Him, for he who comes to God must believe that He is, and that He is a rewarder of those who seek Him" (Hebrews 11:6). Faith—really trusting God—is basic to the Christian life.

Telling. If someone gave you $1,000 and offered to give $1,000 to each of your friends, it wouldn't take you long to tell everyone, would it? But just think, every day your heavenly Father, the Lord of the universe, gives you something worth far more than $1,000. He offers total, unconditional love, full acceptance through Christ, eternal life with Him as His child, plus much more to all who will trust Him. Are you telling anyone?

Enjoying. You can experience a special relationship with all three Persons of the Triune God in community with the other believers in your church and in communion with God in prayer. Allow that truth to soak in next time you hear your pastor conclude a worship service with 2 Corinthians 13:14: "The grace of the Lord Jesus Christ, and the love of God, and the fellowship of the Holy Spirit, be with you all."

Your Turn for Logic and Poetry

Evidence. The Bible never tries to prove God's existence. It just tells *about* Him. Yet, if you think awhile, you can come up with some evidences of God's reality—evidences you can see in nature and in people. Make a list of evidences that prove God's existence.

Risking all or nothing. Blaise Pascal, a 17th century French philosopher and mathematician wrote:

If you live as though there is no God,
and there isn't,
then you've gained nothing and lost nothing.
And if you live as though there *is* a God,
and there isn't,
then you've gained nothing and lost nothing.
But if you live as though there is a God
and there *is*,
then you receive eternal gain.

Does this sound like good logic to you? Discuss why or why not with the members of your group.

Everywhere today. Paraphrase Psalm 139:7-12, using places and situations familiar to 20th century people. Include places close to you as well as distant points in the world and out of this world.

Unbind Your Mind
with these capsule definitions

attribute—a distinctive characteristic

eternal—without beginning or end; existing at all times

hallowed—recognized as holy

holiness—perfection; separation from sin

justice—fairness; moral rightness

omnipotent—all-powerful

omnipresent—in all places

omniscient—all-knowing

redeem—rescue or buy back

righteousness—being just; doing what is right

theology—the study of God

Trinity—tri-unity; God the Father, God the Son, and God the Holy Spirit united as the one God.

4 The Doctrine of Scripture

The word "Bible" comes from the Greek word *biblia*, meaning "books." The Bible is an amazing collection of many books.

Though written by at least 36 different people in many different circumstances, over a 1,500-year period, the 66 books all fit together as the great unfolding revelation of God and His purposes. All the separate books consistently support each other's message even though the writers were unaware, for the most part, of one another's writings.

The terms "Old Testament" and "New Testament" have been used since the close of the second century to distinguish the Jewish and Christian Scriptures. Christians recognize all of the 39 Old Testament books and the 27 New Testament books equally as the Word of God. The New Testament reports and explains fulfillments of the Old and reveals God's new way of life for His people.

Most of the Old Testament was written in the Hebrew language. Most of the New was written in Greek. A few parts of each were written in Aramaic—the language spoken by Jesus. Since then, translators have put all or portions of the Bible into more than 2,000 other languages.

The term "canon" refers to the collection of books officially recognized as the inspired Word of God. All of the Old Testament books had been adopted into the canon before the time of Christ. Most of the New Testament books had been adopted into the canon by A.D. 170, and all 27 were certified by the Council of Carthage in A.D. 397.

Writers of the Bible books didn't know that the words they were writing would become part of the permanent Scriptures to be read by millions of people on every continent for centuries. Each wrote in his own style, for his particular time and circumstance. Yet, whether they were writing intimate messages or public proclamations, God specially guided them. Direct translations of their writings are completely reliable as God's official revelation of Himself and His purpose to all mankind.

Each part of the Bible, and all of it together, is without error in the original manuscripts. The never-ending work of research scholars continually confirms the amazing accuracy of the translations we have now. Meanwhile other scholars, aware of the natural and constant change in languages, are making revisions of the translations. This assures today's readers that they are getting the true meaning of the Scriptures in their own language.

When you read the Bible from cover to cover, the first 17 books are basically the history of the Israeli nation. Then come five books of poetry, each in a different form. They are followed by 17 books by prophets, each with different personalities and emphases, though united in their basic message.

The New Testament starts with four different people's perspectives of the life of Jesus Christ, each helping to round out the whole story of the Gospel for us. Acts, the fifth book of the New Testament, is historical and biographical, starting from Jesus' ascension and running through the early years of the Christian church. Then you get to read 21 pieces of mail originally sent to groups or individuals whose needs and experiences parallel your own life in many ways. The final book in the Bible is the intriguing forecast of Christ's coming kingdom.

The Bible gives us many crucial teachings in simple, direct, unmistakable language. It also reveals many exciting truths in subtler forms, like parables and allegories, that throw curves at the keenest literary minds. God wants us to engage our minds and hearts in deeper study and contemplation of His Word. We must seek the Holy Spirit's help in understanding, interpreting, and experiencing what we read.

Christianity is a testing-and-proving kind of faith. It's not a faith of easy believing. Even in Bible study, if everything were all spelled out for us, we'd have no responsibility but to nod in agreement. God does want us to just agree. More than that, He wants us to understand and put His Word to the test in our lives.

Bible study that links both looking and living is something you can never finish. I know people who insist that though they have studied the Bible daily for decades and have read it through over and over again, they always discover something fresh and useful in it, each and every day. It's full of all kinds of exciting things for us if we approach it openly and responsively, remembering that its essential truth revolves around Christ and that its real interpreter is the Holy Spirit.

Some things the Bible says about itself

Throughout the Old Testament we find claims that God spoke through His human servants. For example, David said: "The Spirit of the Lord spoke by me, and His word was on my tongue" (2 Samuel 23:2). In the New Testament, too, we find many such claims. Paul, in a letter to the Christians of Thessalonica, wrote: "We also constantly thank God that when you received from us the word of God's message, you accepted it not as the word of men, but for what it really is, the word of God which also performs its work in you who believe" (1 Thessalonians 2:13).

Jesus showed His acceptance of the authority of the Old Testament by quoting from it, and making statements directly about it. Once, in front of a crowd, He said, "Do not think that I came to abolish the Law or the Prophets; I did not come to abolish, but to fulfill. For truly I say to you, until heaven and earth pass away, not the smallest letter or stroke shall pass away from the Law, until all is accomplished" (Matthew 5:17-18).

Before His crucifixion Jesus told His disciples plainly that He was to be killed and would rise again in fulfillment of Old Testament prophecy. And after His resurrection He said, in a private meeting with those disciples, "These are My words which I spoke to you while I was still with you, that all things which are written about Me in the Law of Moses and the Prophets and the Psalms must be fulfilled" (Luke 24:44).

A few decades later, in a letter to Timothy, Paul said, "All Scripture is inspired by God and profitable for teaching, for reproof, for correction, for training in righteousness; that the man of God may be adequate, equipped for every good work" (2 Timothy 3:16-17). This principle applies equally to Old and New Testament Scriptures.

The word "inspired" means "God-breathed" and indicates that God is the source of these writings. They are completely reliable. Another important statement about the Bible's real origin appears in a letter from Peter: "Know this first of all, that no prophecy of Scripture is a matter of one's own interpretation, for no prophecy was ever made by an act of human will, but men moved by the Holy Spirit spoke from God" (2 Peter 1:20-21).

Regarding the New Testament, Paul wrote to a church in Greece: "Now we have received, not the spirit of the world, but the Spirit who is from God, that we might know the things freely given to us by God, which things we also speak, not in words taught by human wisdom, but in those taught by the Spirit, combining spiritual thoughts with spiritual words" (1 Corinthians 2:12-13)

What it means

Have you ever heard someone say, "It doesn't matter what you believe as long as you have faith"? That's not very bright, is it? Your faith is only as good as the person or thing in which you place your faith. Some people seem to trust, quite sincerely, in gods that don't even exist. Others place misguided trust in their own ideas of what God is like, not in who He really is. What a tragedy. It matters greatly who and what you believe, not just that you believe *something* and feel good about it.

Even as Christians, it's possible to slide into the error of trying to live on our feelings. That's dangerous. Our feelings are too easily swayed. All sorts of things can give us emotional highs or lows that are entirely unrelated to the fact of our relationship to God. We all need a steadily growing understanding of God's truth. Scripture serves the crucial purpose of clear communications from God. We need the Bible as the basic source of content for our faith.

The Bible is not God's *only* channel for communicating truth about Himself to us. God communicates through creation (Psalm 19:1-2). He communicates through Christians (2 Corinthians 3:2-3). And He has specially communicated through Jesus' life, teachings, death, and resurrection (Hebrews 1:1-2). And the Holy Spirit communicates with those who tune their hearts and minds to what He says. But it is significant that the Holy Spirit, who Jesus said would "guide you into all truth" (John 16:13), generally does so through Scripture.

The Bible does not merely contain the Word of God: It *is* the Word of God. Anyone who says it merely contains God's Word takes on the enormous responsibility of deciding just which parts are from God and which are not. The Bible itself repeatedly indicates that God caused men to write the exact words He wanted them to use, but He also allowed the personality of each writer to come through as part of the message.

When you are reading a book or chapter of the Bible, you can understand it more clearly if you know who the writer was, to whom it was first written, and in what circumstances.

It's also important to notice how any single verse or paragraph or chapter fits into what's been said before and after it. That way you are more likely to understand the true meaning of the separate parts. The concern for correct interpretation of Scripture is called *hermeneutics*. Such carefulness can spare us from false and dangerous conclusions.

What the Bible says about itself adds up to a powerful argument for correctly learning and obeying what it says.

What's the application for you?
Since the Bible is the true guidebook for Christians, everything you, as a Christian, do should be governed by it. What you are to be and do is clearly outlined. You will be held responsible for what you do about it.

If Christians who've studied the Bible every day of their lives still discover new things, what does that suggest about your own Bible reading habits? Worship and fellowship with other Christians are important. So is listening to regular Bible teaching. But nothing can take the place of your own daily study of the Word of God. If you apply yourself to such study, the Lord promises to open and explain His Word to you by the Holy Spirit. A balanced experience of Bible reading and prayer is your main source of strength for both the offensive and the defensive spiritual "warfare" you are constantly fighting in today's world.

I know from personal experience that the seemingly simple practice of daily Bible meditation is something that Satan opposes vigorously. But that simple act of daily meditation is a difficult discipline to learn and practice. Yet the vibrancy of your Christian life depends on it.

The advice of Paul is: "Let the word of Christ richly dwell within you" (Colossians 3:16). To a young man he wrote: "Be diligent to present yourself approved to God as a workman who does not need to be ashamed, handling accurately the word of truth" (2 Timothy 2:15). And to that same young man he also wrote: "Evil men and imposters will proceed from bad to worse, deceiving and being deceived. You, however, continue in the things you have learned and become convinced of, knowing from whom you have learned them; and that from childhood you have known the sacred writings which are able to give you the wisdom that leads to salvation through faith which is in Christ Jesus" (2 Timothy 3:13-15). Sounds like good avice, doesn't it?

John, Paul, Peter, and the other Bible writers advise you to remember one more point. A big point: Scripture is not just for meditation. It's for doing. Here's one sizzling direct quote:

"Prove yourselves doers of the word, and not merely hearers who delude themselves. For if anyone is a hearer of the word and not a doer, he is like a man who looks at his natural face in a mirror; for once he has looked at himself and gone away, he has immediately forgotten what kind of person he was" (James 1:22-24).

Jesus said, "If you love Me, you will keep My commandments" (John 14:15). Obviously He didn't mean that you'll just keep a copy of His commands on a shelf—or even in your mind. He meant that you'll obey His commands. Is that unreasonable or too hard? Not when you consider what He is like, and how ready He is to be your Partner in such living. As the Apostle John said, "This is the love of God, that we keep His commandments; and His commandments are not burdensome " (1 John 5:3).

Not Really a Riddle but it'll make you think!

How to meditate. Psalm 1:2 and Psalm 119:15 talk about *meditating* on Scripture. See what your dictionary says about the word "meditate." Think about those two verses in the Psalms, noting their connection with verses just before them and just after them. Now write a short paragraph telling how you plan to meditate on Scripture during the coming week.

Doing the doing. The expression "doers of the Word" brings up questions about its meaning. Find clues by looking through the whole chapter in which the expression appears (James 1).

Versions. About 370 years ago, 50 scholars working for King James I of England made a Bible translation that's still widely used today. Because of changes in the English language, many other English translations have appeared, especially in this century. Look in copies of several versions and see how each version expresses the same thoughts in different words. Read the same passage in each version, perhaps Psalm 1 or 2 Timothy 3:13-17 or any other passage we've studied in this chapter. Compare also a *paraphrase,* such as *The Living Bible.*

Unbind Your Mind
with these capsule definitions

canon—the Bible; the collection of 66 books which the church officially recognizes as genuinely and uniquely inspired by God

epistle—a letter

heresy—a teaching or opinion that is contrary to what the Bible teaches

illumination—God the Holy Spirit opening our minds and hearts so we can understand the message of the Bible

inspiration—God the Holy Spirit putting His message into the hearts and minds of chosen persons who wrote the Bible books

parable—a story illustrating a spiritual truth

paraphrase—a restatement in familiar, easy-to-understand words; a thought-for-thought translation

prophet—a God-chosen person who foretells things God reveals to him

revelation—something made known by God to man

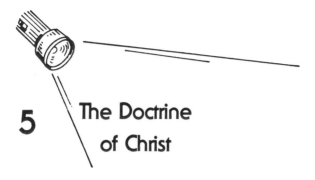

5 The Doctrine of Christ

Christ is the center of the Christian life. He is the greatest gift of God. He is the primary message of Scripture.

If anyone tries to tell you that the center of the Christian life is the church, or the fruit of the Spirit, or selflessness, or the Ten Commandments, or the Golden Rule, he's wrong.

Christ is also the Model of perfection, the only sinless Man who ever lived. By His own choice He took our sins on Himself in order to redeem us and make us like Himself. To be a Christian means to be a "Christ-one"; one whose life is redeemed by and committed to Christ; one who is becoming more and more like Christ.

All His days on earth, Jesus was perfect in all ways. He never sinned. He always did the whole will of God. Our world has never witnessed real perfection outside of Christ. A few gymnasts have been judged "perfect" in some of their events. But their less-than-perfect scores far outnumber the flawless routines. In industry, measures that vary a few thousandths of an inch are called "perfect." But Jesus Christ is absolute and constant perfection in every way, for all time and eternity.

Though many people fail to recognize Him, Christ is God incarnate—God in flesh. He was with the Father and the Holy Spirit at the creation of the world. The Old Testament pointed to His future appearance on earth as the Messiah. The New Testament tells of His earthly ministry and promises His return. He is Lord—recognized or not. And a time will come when everyone *will* see and know Him as Lord (Philippians 2:9-11).

Jesus Christ lives today. He is all-knowing, all-powerful, all-present, caring, watching, loving us, involved with us. He is your gift from God. And the Bible has so much to say about Him that we can only highlight some of it in this book.

William Evans, in his book *The Great Doctrines of the Bible,* quotes Sinclair Patterson on the fact that Christianity is the one faith that cannot survive without its namesake. Buddhist and Muslim doctrines remain intact though their founders are dead. But Christianity without the living Christ is nothing. Our entire faith is built on His life, His death, His resurrection, forgiveness of sins, His continuing work in and through our lives, and His promised return. If He had not been raised from the dead, Christianity would have died.

What the Bible says about Christ

The Bible says Jesus is God. "In the beginning was the Word, and the Word was with God, and the Word was God" (John 1:1).

Right there, John clearly says that Christ is as eternal as God the Father. He was with God the

Father at creation, and He, in fact, is God. This truth is emphasized in some of Jesus' names, such as *Immanuel,* which means "God with us" (Matthew 1:23). In another verse He is called "the true God" (1 John 5:20).

The Bible not only calls Jesus God, but it also attributes to Him the characteristics of God. "Jesus Christ is the same yesterday, today, yes, and forever" (Hebrews 13:8). Not only was He *present* at the time of creation; He also *took part* in it (John 1:3). Read Mark 2:7-12 and you'll see that Christ has God's power to forgive sin.

Unbelievers have sometimes said that Jesus never claimed to be God. To say that, they must ignore the fact that even Christ's enemies understood what He was saying. They accused Him of blasphemy—claiming to be God. He said that He and His Father are one (John 10:30). And He said that whoever had seen Him had seen His Father (John 14:9).

One of the amazing truths about Jesus is that He is *both* God and man. The Person of the Godhead who was with the Father at the creation of the world left His heavenly position to be limited by a human body and become a man. That is the miracle of the incarnation. Jesus willingly put on flesh. He identified Himself with the sin-cursed human race. He had a body that could be killed.

We know Jesus was truly a man for He grew weary, was tempted, became thirsty and hungry. He often called Himself the Son of Man, focusing on the amazing fact of His humanity.

"The Word became flesh and dwelt among us" (John 1:14). What other humility of any kind could compare with Jesus Christ's voluntarily giving up His place in glory to come to earth as a man, to come and die? (Philippians 2:5-8)

Jesus Christ was born of Mary, a virgin—a woman who had never engaged in sexual intercourse. Impossible? Yes, without God. Unique? Absolutely. The reason? If Christ had been born of man's seed, He would have been born in sin just like everyone else. (See chapter 1 about Adam.)

Some people are uncomfortable with the thought of a literal virgin birth. Yet this is one of the cornerstones of our faith. It is essential. If you don't believe that God could and did bring it about, then, in the words of J. B. Phillips, "your God is too small."

In the home of Mary and Joseph, the boy Jesus—playing, laughing and working— "continued to grow and become strong, increasing in wisdom; and the grace of God was upon Him" (Luke 2:40). Human in every way, He also experienced adolescence and entered adulthood —all without sin.

Jesus experienced oppression and rejection. For a while even His brothers didn't believe Him (John 7:5). Some of the neighbors in His small hometown questioned, "Isn't this just Joseph's son?" (Luke 4:22) As the prophet Isaiah had predicted, "He was despised and forsaken of men" (Isaiah 53:3). John said, "He came to His own, and those who were His own did not receive Him" (John 1:11), but those who *did* receive Him became the children of God (1:12).

One reason for His being rejected was that His perfection was just too much for the consciences of those who were self-righteous hypocrites. Any who believed Him had to be willing to confess their own sin and receive Him as their *forgiver*.

Jesus Christ's sinless life was not free from temptation. "We do not have a high priest who cannot sympathize with our weaknesses, but one who has been tempted in all things as we are, yet without sin" (Hebrews 4:15). He understands what we go through in our daily battles with sin.

How humiliating it was for the one perfect, sinless Man of all time to be punished for everyone else's sin. In His death, part of the punishment was that God the Father turned His back on Him (Matthew 27:46). At that time, all our sins were put on His account. The Scriptures say He actually became sin for us (2 Corinthians 5:21).

The same Jesus whose self-sacrifice provides a way of forgiveness for our sin, will someday also be the Judge of all mankind. "Not even the Father judges anyone, but He has given all judgment to the Son" (John 5:22). "When the Son of Man comes in His glory, and all the angels with Him, then He will sit on His glorious throne. And all the nations will be gathered before Him; and He will separate them from one another, as the shepherd separates the sheep from the goats" (Matthew 25:31-32). Jesus, more than anything else, wants to remove our guilt and make us His faithful disciples in this life, rather than judge us as sinners at that time. How important it is for us to come to know Him *now* as our Saviour and Lord, rather than to face Him still in our sins on judgment day.

One of the most beautiful passages about the

sacrifice of Jesus and its right effect on our lives is 1 Peter 2:21-24: "You have been called for this purpose, since Christ also suffered for you, leaving you an example for you to follow in His steps, who committed no sin, nor was any deceit found in His mouth; and while being reviled, He did not revile in return; while suffering, He uttered no threats, but kept entrusting Himself to Him who judges righteously; and He Himself bore our sins in His body on the cross, that we might die to sin and live to righteousness; for by His wounds you were healed."

Jesus died, but He rose again! Without the resurrection of Jesus, we have nothing. A dead Christ would make all the prophecy of Scripture mean nothing and death would be the victor over us all. Christ's resurrection from the dead completed God's transaction with man, won the final victory over Satan, and became the guarantee of the many resurrections which will take place upon His return for His people.

When He ascended to heaven, two angels appeared to His disciples and asked, "Why do you stand looking into the sky? This Jesus, who has been taken up from you into heaven, will come in just the same way as you have watched Him go into heaven" (Acts 1:11). His second coming will be visible, glorious, and unmistakable! You can count on His return—He *is* coming.

What the Doctrine of Christ means

Jesus is God. He has all the characteristics of God. Born of a virgin, He became man. As man He lived a perfect life. He took all our sin on Himself in death, and rose again, just as Old

Testament Scripture predicted. God's visit to this world in the Person of Jesus Christ is the most amazing, fantastic story ever told. It shows that God is truly loving, perfectly righteous, just, and holy. Even His exposure to temptation has great meaning for us. "Since He Himself was tempted in that which He has suffered, He is able to come to the aid of those who are tempted" (Hebrews 2:18).

Christ's birth, life, death, and resurrection prove the faithfulness of God and establish Jesus' supremacy over all the earth. The reconciling work that Christ did for us could be done only by His obeying the will of His Father. He has made all the necessary arrangements for our salvation. Right now, in heaven, He continually prays for us and will do so until He returns to be with us visibly and forever.

By His Spirit, Jesus is also with us right now here on earth. Before He returned to the Father, He told His disciples, "Lo, I am with you always, even to the end of the age" (Matthew 28:20).

When a believer faces physical death, Jesus' resurrection is even more meaningful. His resurrection is the guarantee that we too will live again. "Christ has been raised from the dead, the first fruits of those who are asleep. For since by a man came death, by a man also came the resurrection of the dead. For as in Adam all die, so also in Christ all shall be made alive" (1 Corinthians 15:20-22). That "Resurrection Chapter" of the Bible goes on to say, "O death, where is your victory? O death, where is your sting? The sting of death is sin, and the power of sin is the law; but thanks be to God, who gives us the victory *through our Lord Jesus Christ"* (15:55-57). Easter *really* means something special to those who are believers in the risen Lord. How much it means, they won't even realize till their short life on earth is over.

What does Christ mean to you?

Today all sorts of religions, new and old, are trying to get young people to follow them. They are competing with Christ. A good thought to keep in mind when such groups make their sales pitch is: "For even if there are so-called gods whether in heaven or on earth, as indeed there are many gods and many lords, yet for us there is but one God, the Father, from whom are all things, and we exist for Him; and one Lord, Jesus Christ, through whom are all things, and we exist through Him" (1 Corinthians 8:5-6).

God is as just and righteous and holy as He can be. And He offers to you the gift of Jesus Christ. By your own choice you can receive the most personal, loving, and costly gift ever given to anyone. You are as unworthy as you can be. The decision whether or not to accept it will affect your whole life. What will you do with Jesus? Do you call yourself a Christian? Do you carry His name without ever considering what it all means?

Will you continue in your sin, trying to hide your "secret" sins from Almighty God? Will you insult God by assuming that the One who created the heavens and the earth, the One who provided the perfect and costly means of your salvation, is unable to give you strength to become His kind of person?

Jesus calls you not only to freedom from guilt and to eternal life in heaven, but to a life of radical discipleship here on earth. He has an all-out life of servanthood planned for you to both *suffer* in (with Him) and to *enjoy* more than you could ever enjoy any other kind of life. Are you willing, like the early disciples, to forsake all competing loyalties in order to be and do whatever He wants? Paul's challenge to present your life as "a living and holy sacrifice, acceptable to God" (Romans 12:1) is the natural result of what he had already written about Jesus Christ: He has purchased you with His blood (Romans 5:8-9).

Are you willing to let Jesus Christ be not just *the* Lord, but *your* Lord?

Analyze!

List at least five ways Jesus' humanity is revealed in the Gospels.

List at least five ways His deity is shown in Scripture.

List at least five ways a Christian can be a "Christ-one."

Examine Hebrews 10:26-29. Discuss what it means to "trample under foot the Son of God."

Unbind Your Mind
with these capsule definitions

deity, divinity—God-ness

Godhead—the Trinity: Father, Son, and Spirit

incarnation—becoming flesh; God the Son became flesh without ceasing to be God.

Messiah—"the Anointed One": the Christ promised by Old Testament prophets

reconcile—to bring God and man back together by removing the guilt from believing man

resurrection of Christ—the return to life of Jesus' body, reunited with His spirit, after His body had been dead

Son of Man—a name Jesus used for Himself to emphasize His humanity

virgin birth—Jesus' birth: His mother's pregnancy was produced as a miracle of the Holy Spirit rather than by sexual intercourse.

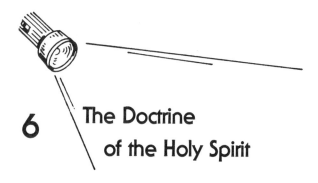

6 The Doctrine of the Holy Spirit

For some reason, people sometimes refer to the Holy Spirit as "it" rather than "He." But the Bible clearly says that the Holy Spirit is God, a *Person*, equal with the Father and the Son.

Bible verses such as Matthew 28:19; John 16:7; 2 Corinthians 3:18; 13:14; and Hebrews 10:15 refer to the Holy Spirit in ways that clearly indicate His personality and deity.

The New Testament describes various ways people can respond to the Holy Spirit. They can lie to Him, blaspheme Him, quench Him, resist Him, grieve Him, yield to Him, honor Him, obey Him, and be filled with Him. These also prove His personhood.

One thing the Holy Spirit does is bring about "conviction of sin." Some would call being "under conviction" a psychological problem. In some cases, this may be true. It's even possible for Satan to counterfeit the conviction of the Holy Spirit to scare someone into running from God or to make him think that he has gotten right with God when he hasn't.

One summer when I was working at a Christian youth camp, a friend of mine came to speak to the campers. He asked me what I thought the kids needed to hear. "There are a lot of phonies here this week," I told him piously.

He preached on 1 Timothy 4:12, about being an "example of the believers" in word and deed. Talk about conviction! The Holy Spirit was really getting through to me. My problem wasn't that I hadn't received Christ. It was that I was not living for Him. Halfway through the sermon, I knew what I had to do. I had to settle things with God.

When my friend gave an invitation to those Christians who wanted to get right with God, I was the first one standing. Knowing that I was a camp worker, he pointed me out as a counselor! I had to counsel the first kid forward while *I* was under conviction.

Somehow I got through the meeting and headed for the privacy of a friend's car. There, I confessed my apathy and determined to live for God. I made promises I knew I would have to keep with the Spirit's help.

While the Spirit still convicts me about my sins and inconsistencies, He does the opposite in relation to my salvation. There He assures me. The Spirit "bears witness with my spirit" that I am a child of God (Romans 8:16). I'm thankful for the Holy Spirit on both counts!

What the Bible says about the Holy Spirit

The Holy Spirit is the Author of the Bible (2 Samuel 23:2; 2 Peter 1:21). He "breathed" the Word of God to the human writers (2 Timothy 3:16). That's important to keep in mind. But there's much more. Before His death, Jesus promised that the Holy Spirit would come as a Helper or Comforter for His people after Jesus' returned to heaven. He explained to His disciples: "I tell you the truth, it is to your advantage that I go away; for if I do not go away, the Helper shall not come to you; but if I go, I will send Him to you. And He, when He comes, will convict the world concerning sin, and righteousness, and judgment; concerning sin, because they do not believe in Me; and concerning righteousness, because I go to the Father, and you no longer behold Me; and concerning judgment, because the ruler of this world has been judged" (John 16:7-11).

The Bible also teaches that the Holy Spirit is the One who gives new life to believers. Most of us have seen people converted to Christ who we thought would never give up their sinful lifestyles. Yet we've seen God working in them through His Holy Spirit, changing them and making them new creatures. This is clear evidence of the work of the Holy Spirit who at the time of our salvation baptizes us into the body of Christ and from that point on lives within us forever.

The Spirit's presence with us makes us God's forever. What a promise! God will stay with us, often in spite of ourselves. We can still quench and grieve His Spirit, but we'll never lose Him.

The Holy Spirit has been active throughout the history of the earth. Before creation "the Spirit of God was moving over the surface of the waters" (Genesis 1:2). From time to time in Old Testament days He was with God's servants to give them the power and wisdom they needed to do the work He had chosen them to do. When David was anointed king of Israel, "the Spirit of the Lord came mightily upon David from that day forward" (1 Samuel 16:13).

We can read a lot about the Spirit's activities during the earthly life of Jesus. It was the Holy Spirit that made it possible for Jesus to be born of the virgin Mary (Matthew 1:20; Luke 1:35). When Jesus was baptized, the Holy Spirit took the form of a dove to show onlookers that He was there (Matthew 3:16, Luke 3:22). It was through the Spirit that Jesus performed His miracles: "If I cast out demons by the Spirit of God, then the kingdom of God has come upon you" (Matthew 12:28).

On the day of Pentecost, however, the Holy Spirit was sent to earth to live permanently in Christians. Ever since Jesus had returned to heaven, His disciples had waited for the Holy Spirit. They knew help was coming, for Jesus had promised that after He left He would send them a Helper. "I will ask the Father, and He will give you another Helper, that He may be with you forever" (John 14:16).

The disciples certainly needed all the help they could get. They were discouraged and powerless. They needed direction. What should they do? Where should they go? Then the Spirit came to them accompanied by tongues of fire and a sudden wind—and He brought power (Acts 2). With the power of God's Spirit, the disciples accomplished great ministries for the good of thousands of people.

Since that time of Pentecost, the Holy Spirit has continued His work here on earth. As He works to glorify Christ, He has some specific tasks to do. If you're a Christian, He has probably touched your life in several areas:

The Spirit witnesses of Christ. As He works to glorify Christ, the Holy Spirit wants people to know exactly who Christ is. "When the Helper comes, whom I will send to you from the Father, that is the Spirit of truth . . . He will bear witness of Me," Jesus told His followers (John 15:26). And later Jesus said of the Holy Spirit: "He shall glorify Me" (John 16:14).

When you heard about Jesus and realized all the wonderful things He had done for you, the Holy Spirit was working in your life. He was glorifying Jesus.

The Spirit lives in believers. If you have accepted Christ, the Holy Spirit lives in you. You are a temple, the temple of God, and within you lives the Spirit of God. Paul said: "Do you not know that you are a temple of God, and that the Spirit of God dwells in you? If any man destroys the temple of God, God will destroy him, for the temple of God is holy, and that is what you are" (1 Corinthians 3:16-17).

Living in us, the Holy Spirit gives us assurance of our salvation: "By this we know that we abide in Him and He in us, because He has given us His Spirit" (1 John 4:13).

Known as the Spirit of truth (John 15:26), the Holy Spirit enlightens our minds as we read the Bible, making truth plain to us. Each time we read the Bible we need to pray something like David did: "Open my eyes, that I may behold wonderful things from Thy law" (Psalm 119:18).

The Spirit guides you as you pray. Do you ever feel like you want to pray about a situation or for a particular person but you're not sure what you should pray for? Don't worry. Pray anyway. The Holy Spirit intercepts our prayers and helps us to pray the right way. "We do not know how to pray as we should, but the Spirit Himself intercedes for us with groanings too deep for words" (Romans 8:26). What a relief! He guides us as we pray. He's even more concerned with our problems than we are.

What does it mean to you?
As you allow the Holy Spirit freedom to work in you, you will begin to see a change in your life. It will come naturally, because the Holy Spirit will be living through you.

When you received Christ as Saviour, several things happened. By your repentance and faith you were made new in Christ. As we have seen earlier, the Holy Spirit was the One who convinced you of sin and led you to Jesus. At the same time, you received what is called the baptism of the Spirit and became a member of God's family. Paul explained it this way: "By one Spirit we were all baptized into one body, whether Jews or Greeks, whether slaves or free, and we were all made to drink of one Spirit" (1 Corinthians 12:13). The "body of Christ" is a term that describes the togetherness of all believers.

True fellowship with other Christians is something all Christians crave. If you like to be with other Christians to share what God is doing and talk about Jesus and life—this is evidence that the Holy Spirit is working in you. When someone is born again, he wants to be with others who know Christ as Saviour and Lord of their lives.

All this is for a purpose. The Holy Spirit wants to achieve certain goals in you as an individual and in the church as a body. He wants you to grow spiritually—becoming more and more like Christ each day, to witness about Jesus, and to obey Jesus in practical ways. And He wants these same things for the church.

In His wisdom the Holy Spirit gives gifts to Christians in order to accomplish His goals for the church. These gifts sometimes appear as talents or abilities, but often they reflect attitudes of the heart. The Apostle Paul listed some for us:

"To each one is given the manifestation of the Spirit for the common good. For to one is given the word of wisdom through the Spirit, and to another the word of knowledge according to the same Spirit; to another faith by the same Spirit, and to another gifts of healing by the one Spirit, and to another the effecting of miracles, and to another prophecy, and to another the distinguishing of spirits, to another various kinds of tongues, and to another the interpretation of tongues. But one and the same Spirit works all these things, distributing to each one individually just as He wills" (1 Corinthians 12:7-11).

As a Christian you have been given at least one from the Spirit. It is your responsibility to recognize and accept your gift and then use it for the benefit of other people.

Sometimes spiritual gifts are misused. One that is often misused is the gift of teaching. The Holy Spirit has given some people the ability to challenge other people's minds. When people with the gift of teaching teach wrong doctrine, they can lead many people from God's truth. Or if they quibble about little silly things, they can take attention away from God and His Word.

You have a responsibility to use your gift or gifts only for the benefit of others, whether it's building up other Christians, or witnessing about Jesus, or serving Him through good works. Gifts are never to be used to make you feel important or superior. The proper use of all gifts leads to spiritual growth in individual Christians and in the church as a whole.

Growth leads to fruit-bearing. Look at this list of good things found in Galatians 5:22-23: "The fruit of the Spirit is love, joy, peace, patience, kindness, goodness, faithfulness, gentleness, self-control." Put all those qualities into a personality and they sound like someone we'd all like to know! But you can be that kind of person if you allow the Holy Spirit to work in your life. It won't happen overnight—or even in a few days or weeks. But you can be changed as you let Him have His way. You see, it's natural to bear fruit. A cherry tree will, by its nature, bear cherries. A Christian will, by his new spiritual nature, bear the fruit of the Spirit.

Remember, the Bible is your guidebook. The Holy Spirit inspired it and He gives you understanding as you read it. The Spirit teaches you through the Bible to avoid sin and to practice love, and then this fruit of the Spirit—love, joy, peace, patience, kindness, goodness, faithfulness, gentleness, self-control—will bud and flower in your life.

The Holy Spirit doesn't want attention for Himself. He wants to glorify Jesus Christ. But when you are aware of the Spirit working in your life, how thankful you are for Him. Ask Him to fill your life every day.

Scripture Self-Study

Fruit of the Spirit. List the fruit of the Spirit identified in Galatians 5:22-23:

love	goodness
joy	faithfulness
peace	gentleness
patience	self-control
kindness	

Alongside each, indicate whether you feel your life is bearing much or little of that particular fruit. Use all nine as a prayer list this week. Keep the list in a place where you'll be reminded of it several times a day.

Unbind Your Mind
with these capsule definitions

baptism of the Spirit—being identified with and united with God in the body of Christ

Comforter—one of the names of the Holy Spirit

conviction of sin—a deep, disturbing awareness of guilt as a sinner separated from God

filled with the Spirit—being completely given to the Holy Spirit for His use

fruit of the Spirit—the cluster of Christlike characteristics the Holy Spirit wants to produce in believers' lives

gifts of the Spirit—special abilities God gives believers to help build and strengthen the body of Christ

intercede—to plead on behalf of someone else

Paraclete—the Holy Spirit; the One "called to the side" of each Christian

prophecy—speaking God's Word to others

regeneration—the Holy Spirit's giving spiritual life to the believer; the new birth

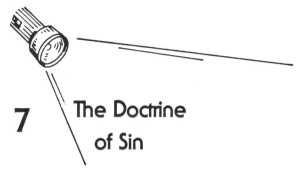

7 The Doctrine of Sin

You can hardly find a clearer single-paragraph definition of sin and sin's origin than the one in *Zondervan's Handy Dictionary of the Bible,* by Merrill C. Tenney. He says:

"Sin is anything in the creature which does not express, or which is contrary to, the holy character of the Creator. The first sin in the universe was an act of free will in which the creature deliberately, responsibly, and with adequate understanding of the issues, chose to corrupt the holy, godly character with which God originally endowed His creation. Sin in the human race had its origin in Adam and Eve (Genesis 3), but sin in the universe had its origin in angelic beings who rebelled against the Creator and whose nature, as a result, became fixed in evil (2 Peter 2:4; Jude 6). Adam and Eve were created with a holy, godly nature, in fellowship with God; as a result of their sin their nature became corrupt; they became hostile to God and guilty before Him; and they involved the whole human race in their corruption and guilt (Romans 5:12-13). The essence of sin is living independently of God. The solution to the problem of sin is found in Christ, in the redemption provided by Him (Romans 3:21—8:39)."

Adam and Eve weren't the first sinners; they were the first *human* sinners. And they certainly weren't the last. Humans have been involved in rottenness ever since—always egged on by the devil and his demons.

After studying all the different Hebrew and Greek words that are translated "sin" in the Bible, a pastor concluded: "Sin is any act or attitude (personal or social) that fails to express love for God, neighbor, or self."

What the Bible says about sin

Warnings about sins against God are represented by the first four of the Ten Commandments (Exodus 20:1-11). Warnings about sins against other people (which are automatically against God too) are represented by the other six (20:12-17).

Jesus summed up all God's commands in this statement: " 'You shall love the Lord your God with all your heart, and with all your soul, and with all your mind.' This is the great and foremost commandment. And a second is like it, 'You shall love your neighbor as yourself' " (Matthew 22:37-39).

The trouble with this simple statement is that not one of us comes close—in fact we miss by a long mile. Sometimes we even have trouble liking our neighbors. That alone makes us sinners!

Not to mention *the Fall*.

We talked about the Fall in the chapter on the doctrine of man. But now as we study the doctrine of sin, let's take another look—this time starting with Tenney's definition in his *Handy Dictionary of the Bible:*

"The fall of man as related in Genesis 3 is the historical choice by which man sinned voluntarily, and thus involved all the human race in evil (Romans 5:12-13; 1 Corinthians 15:22). By the fall, man was alienated from God. Man had been created in God's own image, with a rational and moral nature like God's, with no inner impulse to sin, and with a will free to choose the will of God. Yielding to the outward temptation turned him from God, and created an environment in which sin became a potent factor. Redemption from the fall is accomplished through the second Adam, Jesus Christ (Romans 5:12-21; 1 Corinthians 15:21-22, 45-49)."

We are given the whole stinging story of the Fall in Genesis 3. It was the serpent who talked Eve into defying God. And the temptation actually came from Satan, who either supernaturally appeared in the visible form of a snake or simply spoke through a real snake (Revelation 20:2).

Always cunning and deceitful, Satan used gradually-escalating doubts and misquotation of God's Word to achieve his goal of getting the first generation of mankind to defy God. Result: the human race became a race of sinners, doomed to die. "Through one man sin entered into the world, and death through sin" (Romans 5:12). Then and there they became physically mortal, as well as spiritually dead.

The reality of our inborn sin nature is obvious in verses such as Psalm 58:3, where David says, "The wicked are estranged from the womb; those who speak lies go astray from birth." And in

Psalm 51:5, where he says, "Behold, I was brought forth in iniquity, and in sin my mother conceived me." And we can add these strong statements about the condition of the human heart: "The heart is more deceitful than all else" (Jeremiah 17:9) and "We . . . were by nature children of wrath" (Ephesians 2:3).

Naturally, many people resent the idea of inherited guilt and inherited mortality. "Why should I be held responsible for something that God let someone else do?" But would *they* be free from sin even if God had not allowed sin to enter the world through Adam and Eve?

One thing is certain: God had a good reason for creating man with the ability to sin. It's clear that God put the newly created Adam and Eve in a garden of splendor where their every need was met. And it's clear that He gave them a simple test of obedience and belief. They had total liberty to obey or disobey, to believe or disbelieve, to respond to God with love or to withhold love from Him. God created man for *fellowship,* and fellowship would be impossible with some kind of creature who had no choice but to obey. God could have created any number of beings *programmed* to love, worship, honor, and obey Him. But what would be the point? God wanted love and fellowship from creatures who *wanted* to love and be with Him. Robots could never give Him love and fellowship.

Nearly everyone does a lot of good things in his lifetime. Even the most ungodly people probably do some good things for others. Yet, when we remember that the only true standard of righteousness is Christ Himself, we can see why the

Bible says: "There is none righteous, not even one" (Romans 3:10).

The sins we commit are a result of our sin nature. We sin because we are sinners. That almost makes it sound as if our sin is all Adam's fault. But ask yourself, "Would *I* have withstood the test Adam and Eve faced?" Remember, "All of us like sheep have gone astray, each of us has turned to his own way" (Isaiah 53:6). William Evans explains how Adam's sin affects all of us this way: "All men were in Adam when he sinned. Fallen he, fallen they. Herein lies the truth of the organic unity of the race."

The results of sin include the breaking of our communion with God. It's like after you've displeased your parents or a friend and you are ashamed to look him or her in the eye. The results also include misery on earth—sadness, pain, and trouble (Genesis 3:16-19); death (Romans 6:23); and hell for those who don't re-enter the family of God (Matthew 25:41).

The Bible is explicit about hell, though many people try to write it off. To the question "Why would a loving God allow someone to go there?" the answer is: He allows it only when a sinner chooses to reject the pardon that God freely offers.

How does all this apply to you?
Man's entire nature has been affected by sin. That includes you. Mentally, physically, spiritually, socially, you are incapable of truly loving God "with all your heart, and with all your soul, and with all your mind" (Matthew 22:37) unless you have received Christ into your life—and un-

less you are daily allowing the Holy Spirit to live through you.

"The mind set on the flesh is hostile toward God; for it does not subject itself to the law of God, for it is not even able to do so. Those who are in the flesh cannot please God" (Romans 8:7-8). These verses point out the importance of living "in the Spirit," not "in the flesh."

In *The Great Doctrines of the Bible*, William Evans says that because of the Fall, our understanding is darkened (1 Corinthians 2:14), our minds and consciences are defiled (Titus 1:15), the flesh and spirit are afflicted (2 Corinthians 7:5), the will is enfeebled (Romans 7:18), and we are utterly without the qualities which meet the requirements of God's holiness. In this life you'll always feel those problems. Christians must struggle constantly with sin. We are unable to conquer sin on our own without God's help. Paul confessed that he saw "a different law in the members of my body, waging war against the law of my mind, and making me a prisoner of the law of sin which is in my members. Wretched man that I am! Who will set me free from the body of this death?" (Romans 7:23-24) You too will probably feel that way sometimes. But remember, Paul went on to answer his own question: "Thanks be to God, through Jesus Christ our Lord!" (7:25)

Another apostle wrote, "To one who knows the right thing to do, and does not do it, to him it is sin" (James 4:17). "Ouch!" But all your sins, whether we've done something wrong or *not* done something right, will be forgiven if we practice 1 John 1:9: "If we confess our sins, He is faithful and righteous to forgive us our sins and to cleanse us from all unrighteousness."

Remember, before that verse John wrote, "If we say that we have no sin, we are deceiving ourselves" 1:8). But even before that he said, "If we walk in the light as He Himself is in the light, we have fellowship with one another, and the blood of Jesus His Son cleanses us from all sin" (1:7).

Through His blood God not only cleanses us from sin and guilt, but He also gives us joyful experiences of fellowship and positive, useful service to Him and to other people.

Think Through—and Celebrate!

What similarities do you see between the way temptation came to Eve in the Garden of Eden and the way temptation comes to people today?

Why do some people continue sinning with apparently little fear of God or conviction of their need for salvation?

What is your soundest reason for hope if you are a sinner who recognizes your separation from God?

What advice from Scripture will you take if you are a Christian who knows that you have done something wrong or have not done something you should have?

If you're musical—Set Psalm 32 (a poem on the

joy of being forgiven) to appropriate music.

If you're artistic—Do an abstract drawing representing the forgiveness joy of Psalm 32.

If you're neither—Express the feeling of Psalm 32 in your own words.

Unbind Your Mind
with these capsule definitions

demons—invisible evil spirits who oppose God and work under Satan's direction

depravity—the moral corruption of man

Fall—the event when Adam and Eve sinned voluntarily and involved the entire human race in evil

guilt—deserving of punishment

iniquity—sin; immorality

principalities—powerful angels or demons

Satan—the wicked spirit who first fell into sin and who is the chief enemy of God and man

sin—disobedience to God; rebellion against God

transgression—violation of a law/or command

8

The Doctrine
of Salvation

part 1

"Thanks be to God through Jesus Christ our Lord!" That's Paul's happy answer to his own desperate words: "Wretched man that I am! Who will set me free from the body of this death?" (Romans 7:24-25)

Much of the Bible can be summed up in two simple, yet important, words: sin and salvation. And salvation points directly to Christ, for Scripture tells us, "There is salvation in no one else; for there is no other name under heaven that has been given among men, by which we must be saved" (Acts 4:12).

Salvation is deliverance from condemnation, pardon from guilt. Man without God is dead. Without God's life in us we can't live good, righteous lives. Scripture is full of phrases like "There is none righteous, not even one" (Romans 3:10 and "Our righteousnesses are as filthy rags" (Isaiah 64:6). Sin is a tyrant.

We need more than forgiveness. We need to be delivered from sin's grip on our lives as well as from its guilt. We need not only a change in our legal standing before God but also a change in our character. The work of Christ has changed our standing before God; the work of the Holy Spirit is changing our character.

What the Bible says about salvation

Faith is the major biblical theme in the area of salvation. As sinners we are totally on the receiving end of this faith transaction. Salvation involves only our receiving Christ. "As many as received Him, to them He gave the right to become children of God, even to those who believe in His name" (John 1:12). And according to Isaiah, faith means trusting and resting in the security of God. "The steadfast of mind Thou wilt keep in perfect peace, because he trusts in Thee" (26:3).

I have had particular trouble remembering another important truth about salvation: The work is accomplished by God alone, not in partnership with me. You probably already know the key Bible statement on this: "By grace you have been saved through faith; and that not of yourselves, it is the gift of God; not as a result of works, that no one should boast" (Ephesians 2:8-9).

Paul expanded on this subject when he said: "He saved us, not on the basis of deeds which we have done in righteousness, but according to His mercy, by the washing of regeneration and renewing by the Holy Spirit, whom He poured out upon us richly through Jesus Christ our Saviour, that being justified by His grace we might be made heirs according to the hope of eternal life" (Titus 3:5-7).

Repentance had an important place in believer David's relationship with God. We see it in

Psalm 38:18, where he says, "I confess my iniquity; I am full of anxiety because of my sin." We can see it also in Psalm 51. And in Luke 13:1-5 we see that Jesus was clear on the subject: "Unless you repent, you will all likewise perish."

"Repent, for the kingdom of heaven is at hand," were the words of John the Baptist, the forerunner of Christ (Matthew 3:2). The apostles preached repentance too: "They went out and preached that men should repent" (Mark 6:12).

The word translated "repentance" in the New Testament means *to change the mind.* It indicates changing one's mind about sin, God, and oneself. This change of mind is often accompanied by sorrow, as in the case of Christians who've fallen into sin (2 Corinthians 7:8-11). Repentance is not an act separate from faith, but saving faith includes that change of mind which is called repentance. It means being sorry enough to turn to God for forgiveness and for His power to change your life. A person can be sorry that he got caught, or sorry he's being punished. That's not repentance. Repentance is honest sorrow *over having sinned* and *over grieving God.* It's that kind of sorrow that leads to the turnaround God wants. Through a prophet God said, "*Let the wicked forsake his way,* and the unrighteous man his thoughts; and let him return to the Lord, and He will have compassion on him; and to our God, for He will abundantly pardon" (Isaiah 55:7).

Strange as it may seem, we can't even accomplish repentance on our own. True repentance is made possible by the Holy Spirit. We can't muster up sorry feelings. We can't fool God by saying we're sorry when we aren't. When we are called to repent, only then do we see how bankrupt we really are and we are forced to call on God to perform His work of grace—producing repentance and saving faith in our hearts.

The greatest gift given to the repentant sinner is the Holy Spirit. "Repent, and let each of you be baptized in the name of Jesus Christ for the forgiveness of your sins; and you shall receive the gift of the Holy Spirit" (Acts 2:38).

We must believe in the Lord Jesus Christ to be saved (Acts 16:31). So many people say they can't come to Christ as sinners till they first clean up their acts so they will be presentable. That notion goes against the Bible's teaching that Jesus will receive us just as we are. It's true that we cannot, in ourselves, please Him or measure up to His standard. But our salvation is based on the repentance-producing work of the Spirit that is tied directly with our faith in the saving power of the blood of Jesus Christ.

It is not our faith or our works that save us. It is Christ. Our salvation is based on faith in Christ, not faith in faith.

What does it mean?

Some people think that Christ came and did away with the Law of Moses. No. Actually, Christ fulfilled the Law in person. He, in effect, rewrote the Law, making it even more difficult to obey.

The Old Testament Law stated that we are not to commit adultery or murder. OK. That's not too difficult to avoid. Most of us can handle that. But when Jesus says that *lust* is equal to adultery and *hatred* is equal to murder—I need help! So does everyone I know. These new commandments force us to trust Christ for new life and for the new level of holiness to which He calls us.

One summer at a camp where I worked I noticed a small girl responding to the invitation to receive Christ. She looked familiar to me, and in talking with her I realized that she had come forward to receive Christ the year before, as an eight-year-old.

"Didn't you give your heart to Jesus *last* year?" I asked, preparing to help her find assurance of her salvation.

"Yes, I did," she replied tearfully. "But since then I've borrowed it back a few times."

How often do we do that? We get interested in doing our own things our own ways and we really don't want to be bothered with Jesus. We know the Holy Spirit is with us, yet we sometimes subject Him to involvements (or *non*involvements) that are against His holy will. When the Spirit shakes our consciences awake, we frankly would like to borrow back our hearts for a while so we wouldn't have to feel so miserable about displeasing Him.

But the life of faith is not a life of not doing things. The eleventh chapter of Hebrews lists all kinds of mighty things done by men and women of faith. And that chapter ends with a strong hint that you and I are to add to the list by *our* experiences of active faith!

Evans, in *The Great Doctrines*, says the great question for Christians is not "What can I do?" but rather "How much can I believe?", for all things are possible to the one who believes God (Mark 9:23).

What does it mean to you?

You probably can't remember the first time you heard that Jesus died for you. Perhaps you didn't catch all the details, but you no doubt learned that He died on the cross because He loves you.

Since then you've learned much more about Christ and the Christian life. But perhaps you're saying, "Couldn't God have saved me without someone dying?"

Remember what you've learned about who God is and about who man is. If you compare God and man, you'll realize why Jesus had to die. God is all power, all righteousness, and all love. He is holy. But man is full of sin. In fact, man is in revolt against God. He cannot help himself. So God came to earth in Jesus and provided salvation through His death on the cross. There was no other way possible. And He did it not just for "the world" but for *you*. He'd have come to earth and died for you if you were the only sinner on earth.

When a little boy refused to put away his scattered toys, his big sister taunted him, "You'd better be good or Mom won't love you."

"That's not true!" said their Mom, coming into the room. "I want both of you to be good just because I do love you."

That's the kind of love God has for us. Unconditional love. Love no matter what we are or do. He doesn't stop loving us because we're bad, though in His love He wants us to be good. "God, being rich in mercy, because of His great love with which He loved us, even when we were dead in our transgressions, made us alive together with Christ" (Ephesians 2:4-5).

God does not close His eyes to evil. If He did,

He would be neither righteous nor loving. Paul says that "the wrath of God is revealed from heaven against all ungodliness and unrighteousness of men" (Romans 1:18). So how does God show His love for us? "God demonstrates His own love toward us, in that while we were yet sinners, Christ died for us" (Romans 5:8).

"Greater love has no one than this," Jesus once said, "that one lay down his life for his friends" (John 15:13). He expressed His love by dying for His friends—and for His enemies as well! The story of that supreme demonstration of love takes two chapters in each of the four Gospels. Read all four accounts thoughtfully: Matthew 26—27; Mark 14—15; Luke 22—23; John 18—19.

Jesus died for you. He suffered for your sins as if you were the only person in the world. He who was perfectly sinless became your substitute. "For Christ also died for sins once for all, the just for the unjust, in order that He might bring us to God" (1 Peter 3:18).

A pointed question strikes you when you read Romans 2:4: "Do you think lightly of the riches of His kindness and forbearance and patience, not knowing that the kindness of God leads you to repentance?"

And this question hits you between the eyes when you read Hebrews 2:3: "How shall we escape if we neglect so great a salvation?"

Two Narrative Think-Throughs

The best-known story that illustrates repen-

tance is Jesus' parable of the prodigal son (Luke
15:11-32). In that story what do you learn
   —about the nature of repentance?
   —about God's response to people who repent?

A true story that illustrates faith is the account
of Peter walking on water (Matthew 14:22-32). In
that account, what do you learn
   —about the nature of faith?
   —about Jesus' relationship with people who
   exercise faith?

Unbind Your Mind
with these capsule definitions

assurance of salvation—inner certainty that you have eternal life

believer—one who belongs to Jesus Christ through faith in Him and His death and resurrection

born again—spiritually alive by the power of the Holy Spirit

confess Christ—to openly tell others about your faith in Christ and your identification with Him

confess sin—to admit your sin to God with sincere sorrow and sincere desire not to repeat it

consecrate—to set apart for God

disciple—a faithful learner; a trusting, obedient follower of Jesus Christ

faith that saves—completely trusting Jesus Christ for your salvation from sin

grace—undeserved favor

pardon—forgiveness

regeneration—given new life by the Spirit

repentance—a change of mind and heart about sin; a turning from sin and a turning to God

righteousness—rightness; free from sin

justification—declared righteous; free from sin

salvation—being rescued from sin; being delivered from condemnation; being brought into a right relationship with God

unregenerate—spiritually dead in sin

9

The Doctrine
of Salvation
part 2

Too many Christians don't know any more about what their salvation is all about than what's in the previous chapter. True, that's all you need to know to be saved. You don't have to be a Bible scholar to experience salvation. But many Christians think that words and concepts, like those listed at the end of the chapters in this book, are just big theological terms that mean nothing to them or their lives.

I was guilty of this as a Christian for a long time. I went to church almost every Sunday and heard all the big words. I figured that if they were really important I'd learn more about them someday. I only wish now that I had studied them earlier. No, they don't make me any more saved. But they give me a much clearer understanding and deeper feeling for what Christ did for me, what He is still doing, and why.

What the Bible says about the salvation work of Christ

An Old Testament symbol for the crucifixion of Christ is the Day of Atonement. *Halley's Bible Handbook* points out that for the Children of Israel, the ceremony on the Day of Atonement, the most solemn day of the year, made them clean before God from the sins of that year (Leviticus 16:30). In the ceremony, the High Priest laid his hands on a sacrificial goat, confessing over it the sins of the people. Then the goat was sent out into the lonely wilderness, carrying away with it the sins of the people (16:21-22). What a picture of the then-future and now-final atonement for sin when Jesus took the world's sins on Himself on the Cross.

Jesus' sacrificial death, pointed to by many of the ceremonial sacrifices of the Old Testament, is the central message of the New Testament.

Many great world leaders have been honored for their lives. But no one in history can be as honored for His death as is Jesus Christ. Though He was the world's greatest teacher and example, He was above all the Redeemer and Saviour by the sacrifice of His life blood for His friends and enemies. He came to earth specifically to die (Matthew 20:28).

One Scripture statement that gives the reason for His becoming man and dying is Hebrews 2:14: "Since then the children share in flesh and blood, He Himself likewise also partook of the same, that through death He might render powerless him who had the power of death, that is, the devil."

Paul's brief but complete summary of the Gospel of Jesus Christ (1 Corinthians 15:1-4) emphasizes the fact that "Christ died for our sins."

In John's remarkable prophecy he said that the song of the redeemed in heaven will have as its theme the death of Christ (Revelation 5:8-12).

Christ's resurrection completed God's transaction with mankind and proved the superiority of God over sin and death. But it was the death of Christ that paid the price of our salvation.

Most theologians agree that the death of Christ is described in the Scriptures by four basic words: (1) ransom; (2) propitiation; (3) reconciliation; and (4) substitution. Let's look at these one at a time.

1. *Ransom* in the Bible means much the same as it does today: to free from captivity or punishment by paying a price. Jesus said of Himself, "The Son of Man did not come to be served, but to serve, and to give His life a ransom for many" (Mark 10:45). Hostage-holding terrorists send ransom notes demanding payment of a ransom. Ransom payments "buy back" the hostages. Some Bible students say that Christ's death paid a ransom to *Satan* for sinners who were bound by him. Others say that Christ paid the ransom to *God*, the Lawgiver. Both interpretations are debatable. Regardless, Scripture is clear that Christ paid the high price of our ransom to set us free from sin and death with His own pure blood.

2. In simplest terms, *propitiation* means satisfaction. In Scripture it means satisfying God's holy law by an offering or sacrifice. God's justice and righteousness must be satisfied for Him to forgive and pardon our sins. Christ's death provided the satisfactory covering for our sins before the holy God. "He Himself is the propitiation for our sins; and not for ours only, but also for those of the whole world" (1 John 2:2).

3. *Reconciliation* means the healing of the broken relationship or the settling of a long dis-

pute between God and man. Our reconciliation with God is made possible by the death of Christ. Paul says, "God was in Christ reconciling the world to Himself" (2 Corinthians 5:19). With the barriers broken and destroyed, the opposite sides can reach out to each other. The holy and righteous God can be touched by any man who has been redeemed and reconciled by the death of Jesus.

4. The word *substitution* is self-explanatory. Jesus died in your place. He's your substitute. Had He not died, everyone on earth would face eternal death. "The Lord has caused the iniquity of us all to fall on Him" (Isaiah 53:6).

Ransom. Propitiation. Reconciliation. Substitution. Each word helps us appreciate more about Christ's death, an event which makes far more difference to us—now and forever—than we'll ever fully realize in this life.

What it means to you

Four more heavy words that help us understand more about salvation are: (1) *regeneration;* (2) *justification;* (3) *adoption;* and (4) *sanctification.* These words describe what happens to a person when he receives Christ.

1. *Regeneration* means rebirth, the new birth or being born again. Jesus told Nicodemus that unless a person is born again, he can't even see the kingdom of God (John 3:3). But in the same Gospel we're told, "As many as received Him (Christ), to them He gave the right to become children of God" (John 1:12). Peter said that we "become partakers of the divine nature" (2 Peter 1:4). We have, as Evans points out, received a

new nature. As Christians, we now possess two natures—the old and the new. The two get into conflict at times, but through conscious use of the Holy Spirit's power, our new nature can defeat the sin-bent old nature.

2. *Justification* means a change in our status before God. We've been declared righteous. We could never stand before God in our sin. But once we receive Christ, God looks at us through His perfect Son and sees us as being as righteous as He is. In His act of justification, God has cast all our "sins into the depths of the sea" (Micah 7:19). He forgives us completely. He literally forgets our transgressions. We become full-fledged children of God, totally *accepted* by the heavenly Father.

3. *Adoption* means to be taken by choice into a relationship. When we are adopted into God's family, we are chosen by Him for that position as a member of His household. While justification gives us a new status with God, our adoption places us in a position to enjoy the benefits of being genuine members of God's family. Scripture explains it this way: "In love He predestined us to adoption as sons through Jesus Christ to Himself, according to the kind intention of His will" (Ephesians 1:4-5). Through that adoption we have become "heirs of God and fellow-heirs with Christ" (Romans 8:17).

4. *Sanctification* differs from the other benefits of salvation because it is not what God does *for* us, but what He does *in* us. It's the process of being made more and more like Christ. Sanctification begins when we are born again and continues until our earth life is completed.

Paul once wrote, "May the God of peace Himself sanctify you entirely" (1 Thessalonians 5:23). Peter encouraged some other Christians by writing about "the sanctifying work of the Spirit" in their lives (1 Peter 1:2). But we must have a part in the process too.

We must willingly and actively enter into what God wants to do in us. He is the source of strength, but we must cooperate. The extent of our sanctification will depend on how much we join our minds and hearts and wills with His—seeking the holiness and obedient servanthood of Christ.

We must also study the Scriptures and obey them—this includes fleeing the lusts of the flesh and of the eyes, and pride (1 John 2:15-17).

The Word of God will help us become more like Christ, as much as we allow it to. And it will help us add "serving faith" to our "saving faith."

Theology Think-Through

Test yourself. In your own words, explain the biblical meaning of propitiation. Then check back in this chapter to see how close you came.

Try another. Reconciliation.

Now try each of the four words in the "What it means to you" section of the chapter: Regeneration. Justification. Adoption. Sanctification.

For further clarification of these words talk with your teacher or your pastor.

Unbind Your Mind
with these capsule definitions

adoption—God's choosing repentant, believing sinners as members of His family

atonement—"at-one-ment"; being brought back into a harmonious relationship

conversion—to change one's direction

expiate—to pay the penalty for sin

holy—perfect; separated from sin

Lamb—symbol for Jesus Christ that emphasizes His sacrifice for our sins

propitiate—to satisfy God's holy law; to cover

reconcile—to make compatible; to restore a harmonious relationship

redeem—to buy back; to rescue from bondage

saint—a person set apart by God for His service (Every Christian is actually a saint even if he doesn't act that way.)

sanctify—to set apart; to make holy; to cleanse from sin

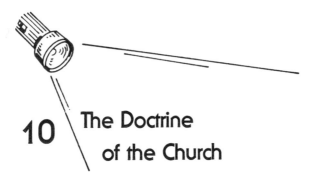

10 The Doctrine of the Church

When you sit through long, unexciting church services or encounter phonies and plastic saints in your church, you may think you can be a better Christian on your own, without the bother of the church.

I felt that way once. And I told my father about it. "The sermons are boring, the music's too slow, and the people—at least some of them—are gossips and hypocrites." I wanted to turn my back on the whole thing and never return.

My dad's reply surprised me. "OK, turn your back on it," he said. "But first give it another chance. Why don't you check it out and see why the church continues in spite of its faults?"

I agreed that I would.

"While you're investigating the church," he added, "why don't you investigate the claims of Christ on your own life? You know where to find them."

So I read the New Testament. As I learned more about God's promise of an abundant life, I challenged God to give me that kind of life. I decided to seek God and ask Him to reveal more of Himself and His ways to me. I was convinced that God wouldn't turn His back on anyone who was sincerely seeking Him.

God didn't turn His back on me. He found me. And I found abundant life in the very church I thought I couldn't stand. The boring sermons became the meat of the Word that I had not been ready for earlier. And most of the people I thought were hypocrites were just older versions of me. They weren't going to church to show people how good they were; they were going because they knew better than anyone else how good they weren't.

The biggest change in my attitude was toward the music. I started to like and appreciate the old hymns. I started thinking of the words as I sang along with the congregation, and I discovered that they expressed my own thoughts of worship beautifully.

As I matured, my church became a focal point for my spiritual growth. I found it hard to imagine how I could survive spiritually without it. The church is not just a man-made institution. Anyone who dares study what the Scriptures say about the church will see that it was established by God. The church is His instrument for reaching out and nurturing people in the faith today.

What the Bible says about the church

You often hear people say that the church is not a building. True. It's not. And yet the Bible uses that same metaphor (among others) to describe the church of God (1 Corinthians 3:9). It calls Christ the cornerstone, the prophets and apostles the foundation, and all Christians "living stones" in that building (1 Peter 2:5). Paul, in a letter to

one church, calls the people "fellow-citizens
with the saints, and . . . of God's household, having been built upon the foundation of the apostles and prophets, Christ Jesus Himself being the
cornerstone, in whom the whole building, being
fitted together is growing 'into a holy temple in
the Lord; in whom you also are being built together into a dwelling of God in the Spirit"
(Ephesians 2:19-22).

What we mean when we say that the church is
not a building is that the church is *people*. Plain,
ordinary—but redeemed—people, united for
worship, fellowship, mutual strength, witness,
and ministry to others. The church you go to is
only a small part of the complete body of believers all over the world. Perfect? Far from it. Yet the
church is part of the kingdom of God.

The best short definition of the church I've
found is: "The church is a body of believers who
have been called out of the world, and who are
under the authority of Jesus Christ." The best
book to study and learn what the church is all
about and what it can be like is the Book of Acts.
Important information is given in the Gospels too.

We know that Jesus Christ is the Head of the
church, because He announced the coming of the
church and said that *He would build it* (Matthew
16:16-18).

The Apostle Paul, after admitting that his
greatest sin before his conversion had been to
persecute the church, considered his most important ministry building up the church. Later he
said, "I am the least of the apostles, who am not
fit to be called an apostle, because I persecuted
the church of God" (1 Corinthians 15:9).

Paul knew Christ's plan for building and completing the church. He told the Christians at Ephesus that Christ assigned special tasks to some believers "for the equipping of the saints for the work of service, to the building up of the body of Christ; until we all attain to the unity of the faith, and of the knowledge of the Son of God, to a mature man, to the measure of the stature which belongs to the fullness of Christ" (Ephesians 4:12-13).

What it means

With Christ as the head of the church and the Source of its life, the church is much more than an organization. It is an organism—a living thing—that must function and grow.

God made everyone with a need to be with other people and to do things together. People form groups to do everything from acrobatics to banjo playing. Christians also need to get together with others of the same mind. And God planned for us to do just that—for our own sakes and for His.

After the first Pentecost feast day following Jesus' ascension, 3,000 Christians were drawn together and were called a church—"the church in Jerusalem" (Acts 8:1). After that group had grown to 10,000 or more, city leaders began to oppose them, just as they had opposed Jesus. They jailed Peter and John for a night. They stoned Stephen to death. Christians fled the city. Some who left Jerusalem settled in Antioch and there they established another church (Acts 11:19-26).

During all of history since that time, many

more churches have started—groups of believers in all countries meet together for worship and mutual strength and witness. The Book of Acts gives us short, lively sketches of many churches. Most of the Epistles are letters sent to churches. Sometimes those groups of believers met in Jewish synagogues, but more often they simply met in homes. What made them churches was not their meeting place but their common commitment to the One in whose name they met.

The New Testament tells us that the churches were made up of believers. "The Lord was adding to their number day by day those who were being saved" (Acts 2:4-7). Holding their first meetings in the Jewish Temple, the Jerusalem Christians were baptized, taught each other, prayed together, observed the Lord's Supper, shared their possessions with any who were in need, and worked for God together (Acts 2:41-47). And the number of believers kept increasing. The Book of Acts tells briefly but breathtakingly how people turned to Christ in other cities— Lystra, Derbe, Philippi, Corinth, Ephesus—and how Paul ministered to the churches in each city.

Worship was always a vital part of their time together. And witnessing (through deeds as well as words) was a vital part of their daily life among their neighbors. They didn't forget what Jesus said just before He returned to heaven: "Go therefore and make disciples" (Matthew 28:19) and "You shall be My witnesses both in Jerusalem, and all Judea and Samaria, and even to the remotest part of the earth" (Acts 1:8).

In their work as well as in their worship, the early Christians felt a strong sense of belonging to each other. They knew what Paul meant when he talked about "teaching and admonishing one another with psalms and hymns and spiritual songs, singing with thankfulness in your hearts to God" (Colossians 3:16). They also knew, from personal experience in hardships and temptations, what he meant when he said, "Brethren, even if a man is caught in any trespass, you who are spiritual, restore such a one in a spirit of gentleness; looking to yourselves, lest you too be tempted. Bear one another's burdens, and thus fulfill the law of Christ" (Galatians 6:1-2).

The special Greek word used in the New Testament for this sense of oneness and concern for each other is *koinonia*—a very special kind of fellowship (Acts 2:42, 1 John 1:3, 7).

Two special ceremonies clearly and boldly announced the church members' identification with Christ. The first, baptism, identified them with the death and resurrection of Christ and was a picture of their being "dead to sin, but alive to God" (Romans 6:11). As Paul said, "We have been buried with Him through baptism into death, in order that as Christ was raised from the dead through the glory of the Father, so we too might walk in newness of life" (Romans 6:4). New believers were usually baptized as a public testimony of their faith.

The other ceremony was the Lord's Supper. Everyone ate from the same loaf of bread and drank from the same cup of wine, symbolizing the body and blood of Christ, given on the cross for their salvation. This practice was patterned after the meal Jesus had with His disciples just before His crucifixion. He told them, "This is My blood of the covenant, which is to be shed on behalf of many for forgiveness of sins" (Matthew 26:28). Paul taught churches to continue celebrating the Lord's Supper, "for as often as you eat this bread and drink this cup, you proclaim the Lord's death until He comes" (1 Corinthians 11:26).

The New Testament stresses the equality of all believers. It teaches that in the church each believer is a *minister*—not in the sense of the professional clergy but in the sense of helping others who are in need.

Pastors (also called bishops, elders, and overseers) are to teach and preach. Paul urged a young pastor by the name of Timothy, "Preach the word; be ready in season and out of season; reprove, rebuke, exhort, with great patience and instruction" (2 Timothy 4:2). Pastors are also to "shepherd" people. That means to guide them by counseling and by example and to see that the sick, the old, and the troubled are cared for. Paul warned church leaders, "Be on guard for yourselves and for all the flock, among which the Holy Spirit has made you overseers, to shepherd the church of God which He purchased with His own blood" (Acts 20:28).

Another category of church ministers given in the Bible is deacons. The word deacon means servant. Deacons are to assist the pastors in serving the needs of fellow believers so that the pastors can concentrate more of their time on their special responsibilities. The way the word is used in Scripture means that all believers are deacons. God's high standards of morality for both pastors and deacons are spelled out in 1 and 2 Timothy and in Titus.

What it means to you

Each local church is to be a united group of redeemed people who are also a worshipping people, a caring people, and witnessing people. If you are a Christian, you are a member of the church, and you should take part in worship, in caring ministries, and in witnessing.

The last two chapters of the Bible contain references to the church as the Bride of Christ. This is an exciting metaphor that pictures the joy which the entire church will experience when Christ, the Bridegroom, comes to take all believers from the sin-cursed world to the home He has prepared in heaven. When that happens, you—if you are a Christian—will know the *full* meaning of being redeemed. But until that happens, you can experience and enjoy an increasing understanding of God's grace in the worshiping/caring/witnessing fellowship of fellow believers in your local church.

Let's all follow Paul's advice: "Let us consider how to stimulate one another to love and good deeds, not forsaking our own assembling together, as is the habit of some, but encouraging one another; and all the more, as you see the day drawing near" (Hebrews 10:24-25).

Not Really Riddles
but you'll have to think!

After carefully checking the story about the beginning of the church (Acts 2), write the account in newspaper style as if it were happening today.

Tell several important ways that God expects the church to be different from any other group of people.

In your own words, list the qualifications for deacons in 1 Timothy 3:8-13.

Name several specific ways that you and other Christians can share in the life and outreach of your church this year.

Unbind Your Mind
with these capsule definitions

apostle—a person who had seen Jesus and was chosen to be a key witness for Him

ascension of Christ—Jesus' physical departure from earth to heaven after His resurrection

church—all true believers in Christ

commission—a responsibility given to someone

communion—the close sharing of thoughts and feelings

corporate worship—a group of believers worshiping God together

heresy—false teaching

hypocrite—a person who pretends to have beliefs or virtues that he doesn't have

koinonia—the special fellowship Christians have with each other

Lord's Supper—believers reverently eating bread and drinking wine together as a symbol of Christ's death

mediator—peacemaker; one who brings separated people together

ministry—giving yourself in loving service to God and others

ordain—to appoint; establish

ordinance—a ceremony or ritual prescribed by God

Pentecost—a Jewish feast day; in New Testament times, the word Pentecost referred to the coming of the Holy Spirit

priest—one who has the privilege and duty of speaking directly to God

prophet—a foreteller or forthteller appointed by God to deliver special messages

stewardship—the wise use of all that God has entrusted to us, such as time, talents, money

tithe—one-tenth of a person's income; money given to God as an act of worship

witnessing—telling and showing others who Jesus Christ is

worship—honoring God; focusing attention on all His divine qualities

11 The Doctrine of Angels

Being a super-active kid, I became restless and depressed when a serious illness kept me in bed for several weeks. I remember lying awake at night when the whole house was dark and quiet. "I can't sleep," I complained. "I want to get up!" One of my mother's ways of quieting me and reassuring me was to sing softly, *"God will take care of you. Beneath His wings of love abide. God will take care of you."*

Too young to understand exactly what those words meant, I was quite content to relax with the thought that God had assigned a winged angel to stand guard at the foot of my bed. It was a nice safe feeling. But I didn't learn what the Bible really teaches about angels till a long time afterward.

The Bible makes many references to angels, who are a lot better than the Anaheim, California baseball team. And they're created for much more important reasons than entertainment.

Angels were specially created by God. They are not glorified humans. They are not spirits of departed Christians. They are a special order of living beings. "For in [Christ] all things were created, both in the heavens and on earth, visible and invisible" (Colossians 1:16).

Angels are for real. But they are in a different dimension of creation than we are. They are superior to earthly man. God made man "for a little while lower than the angels" (Hebrews 2:7). But angels are people-helping spirits. "Are they not all ministering spirits, sent out to render service for the sake of those who will inherit salvation?" (Hebrews 1:14)

Gifted with many special abilities, angels can shuttle from heaven to earth and back again in a flash—unhindered by walls, gates, or doors. They don't have physical bodies. Yet at special times they can and do become visible to fulfill some errand for God.

Angels don't grow old. They don't die. The angel Gabriel, who appeared to Daniel (Daniel 8:16; 9:21), also appeared to Mary (Luke 1:26-27)—six centuries later. Angels have great strength. They are "greater in might and power" than humans (2 Peter 2:11). But they don't all have equal authority. Michael is named as an *arch*angel—one with authority over many angels (Jude 9). In *Great Doctrines,* Evans says that angels "are mighty but not almighty." And though they have superhuman abilities, angels don't know everything. They're not omniscient. Jesus, when telling His disciples about His future return to earth, said, "But of that day and hour no one knows, not even the angels of heaven" (Mark 13:32). And Peter, writing of the deep truths about salvation, said there were "things into which angels long to look" (1 Peter 1:12).

There are a lot of angels. Ten thousand of them were at Mount Sinai when God gave the Law to Moses (Deuteronomy 33:2). "A multitude of the heavenly host" appeared at the birth of Christ (Luke 2:13). And in a report of his vision of the still-future revelation of Christ, John wrote, "I looked, and I heard the voice of many angels around the throne . . . and the number of them was myriads of myriads, and thousands of thousands" (Revelation 5:11).

Some Old Testament passages, such as Genesis 16:7-13, tell about people's conversations with "*the* angel of the Lord." That generally means they were talking to God Himself. Such appearances of God are called *theophanies*. A theophany is somewhat similar to a visit of an angel, but it's different in that "*the* angel of the Lord" speaks with His own full authority. Angels only deliver messages *for* God. They have no authority of their own.

Angels are not imaginary creatures out of children's stories. They're not some kind of winged delivery men or feminine detectives. They're spirits in the service of their Creator. They do things for us that we don't even know about. And when they do something visible, it's never to draw attention to themselves but to bring honor to God.

Jesus was aware of angels while He was on earth, but He never called on them for a "show." When He was so hungry in the desert Satan tried to get Him to do a stunt with angels. Quoting a psalm which says, "He will give His angels charge concerning you; and on their hands they will bear you up" (Matthew 4:6), Satan urged

Jesus to dive off the pinnacle of the temple. That would have been a spectacular show, but Jesus knew that angels were created for holier purposes.

Even on the night that Jesus was arrested, when Peter impulsively swung a sword and sliced off a soldier's ear, Jesus said He could have the help of 12 legions of angels (72,000) if He wanted to (Matthew 26:53). But He *did not.* His concern was not supernatural protection, but doing the will of God. That should be our attitude too. We receive God's supernatural protection from physical injury and death many times. But God sometimes does allow His people to experience physical harm or even to be killed, things we'll understand in eternity if not now.

Angels are sometimes called *heralds* because they announce news. They make both private and public announcements. A private message was given to Joseph, telling him not to be afraid to take Mary as his wife (Matthew 1:20-21). A more public announcement was made to shepherds near Bethlehem (Luke 2:9-15).

Angelic announcements have been given at highly dramatic moments. Like the morning of Jesus' resurrection when the angel who rolled the stone away from His tomb said to the two women: "Do not be afraid; for I know that you are looking for Jesus who has been crucified. He is not here, for He has risen, just as He said" (Matthew 28:5-6).

Another highly dramatic moment was when two angels appeared to the apostles right after Jesus had ascended to heaven, and said, "Why do you stand looking into the sky? This Jesus, who has been taken up from you into heaven, will come in just the same way as you have watched Him go into heaven" (Acts 1:11).

A *not*-so-beautiful situation to which an angel came was when Peter was chained between two guards, in a prison cell—condemned to be executed. Imagine Peter's feelings when an angel woke him up, his chains fell off, and the angel led him out to freedom (Acts 12:5-11).

Angels can't be witnesses about salvation. But they sometimes help bring a witnessing Christian and a seeker together. In Acts 8, an angel directed a Christian to a seeker, Philip to an Ethiopian. And in Acts 10 it was the other way around. The seeker was directed to a Christian, Cornelius to Peter. Both of those angel-directed contacts led to conversions. But in both instances the actual witnessing was done by humans.

Angels are involved in some unpleasant missions too. They were responsible for the extinction of 185,000 enemies of David (2 Kings 19:32-35). And at the end of the age, they will effect the punishment of the wicked (Matthew 13:49-50).

Speaking of the wicked and punishment, hell is the place prepared for the devil and his angels—angels who have fallen because they rebelled against God. "God did not spare angels when they sinned, but cast them into hell and committed them to pits of darkness, reserved for judgment" (2 Peter 2:4). "Angels who did not keep their own domain, but abandoned their proper abode, He has kept in eternal bonds under darkness for the judgment of the great day" (Jude 6).

Fallen angels are enemies of God, battling in a

struggle with the forces of God for dominance and power. Their evil activities will end at the day of judgment. Meanwhile, "Our struggle is not against flesh and blood, but against the rulers, against the powers, against the world-forces of this darkness, against the spiritual forces of wickedness in the heavenly places" (Ephesians 6:12).

While demons fight against us in that warfare, God's holy angels help us. The Bible tells us much more about God's angels than about Satan and his, because God's forces will win in the end. And they can win in our day-by-day battles as we commit our lives to God's will.

What it means to you

You have unlimited resources from God to help you live the Christian life. You don't need to ask for a guardian angel to follow you around; you already have one. Maybe more than one. You don't need to pray to angels, because God assigns them when and wherever He sees that we need them.

It's important to clear your mind of any unbiblical images you might have of angels. They don't lounge around on clouds playing harps. Scripture indicates that angels are neither male nor female. Since our minds are not equipped to visualize spirits, it seems that we would do well to picture them as strong, bold beings, capable of whatever great missions God assigns to them.

While working in a Christian youth camp as a teenager, I happened to be walking a few steps behind the week's featured speaker when she suddenly began talking. No one else was around. I quickened my pace and got closer, only to hear her say, "Sorry, angels."

I was shocked. I thought the lady had gone bananas. She repeated her apology, "Sorry, angels." Then she saw me and smiled.

It was not the smile of a crazy woman. Seeing the look on my face, she didn't even wait for me to ask what in the world she was talking about. "I sometimes feel sorry for the angels," she said. "For some reason God has not chosen them to take part in His forgiveness and salvation. They miss out on something I have. Sorry, angels. When I see these children here at camp coming to Jesus, I know the angels rejoice with me. But I realize that going from darkness to light, from death to life, from punishment to glory, is something that the angels can never really understand."

I will never forget that lesson. Our experience of redemption is something unique that angels will never experience.

But the angels are on our side. In all kinds of circumstances, we can look to the Holy Spirit Himself for comfort and instruction, *and* we can know that His angels will add protection and a boost when we need it.

The study of angels should also prompt us to be kind and thoughtful to strangers. An intriguing verse of Scripture says, "Do not neglect to show hospitality to strangers, for by this some have entertained angels without knowing it" (Hebrews 13:2).

We are never to worship angels (Colossians 2:18). But we are to worship the God who created both them and us—and who sometimes uses them to help us in our lives.

Not Really Riddles

List some of the most important messages that angels have ever brought to people from God as told in the Old and New Testaments.

Does the doctrine of angel protection mean that Christians may be careless—for example, when swimming or when driving a car—and not worry about getting hurt?

What will angels be doing when Christ is revealed in all His power and glory? (Revelation 5:11-14)

Unbind Your Mind
with these capsule definitions

angels—supernatural beings; spirits created a little higher in dignity than man, who serve God in heaven and on earth as "ministering spirits"

archangel—an angel or other higher spirit with authority over many angels

heavenly host—all the angels of heaven

theophany—the brief appearance of God in the form of a person or an angel, sometimes called "*the* angel of the Lord"

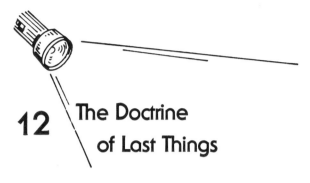

12 The Doctrine of Last Things

Choose any superlative you can think of. It will fit this doctrine. It's complicated, mysterious, exciting, fantastic.

If you aren't convinced by now that the Bible is true and is meant as God's message to you, this chapter will have little impact on you. The doctrine of last things is foolishness to those who don't believe. It's bizarre even to the believer. But what intriguing experiences are in store for us! And what an encounter we'll have with the living God Himself!

The doctrine of last things involves so many different events that it's often misunderstood. And God purposely keeps us in the dark about some points. But that shouldn't make us shrug our shoulders, as some people do, and just figure we'll see how it all comes out in the end. Certain parts of eschatology (the study of last things) are clear in Scripture, and are important to know and live by. That's why God put them there.

What the Bible says about last things

Shortly before He was crucified, Jesus told His

disciples, "I go to prepare a place for you. And if I go and prepare a place for you, *I will come again,* and receive you to Myself; that where I am, there you may be also" (John 14:2-3). That place He went to prepare was heaven—the special dwelling place of God and His followers.

Jesus' "coming again" is not merely His coming for Christians at their death. It is His future visible return to earth to take all His people to be with Him forever. Theologians call it the rapture.

Paul wrote: "Our citizenship is in heaven, from which also we eagerly wait for a Saviour, the Lord Jesus Christ; who will transform the body of our humble state into conformity with the body of His glory, by the exertion of the power that He has even to subject all things to Himself" (Philippians 3:20-21).

From verses like these we see that we who are Christians are already citizens of heaven, though we're still citizens of earth too. When we make the move, we ourselves will be changed, to have heaven-oriented bodies. Our bodies will be totally renewed. Though we'll retain our identities, we'll be permanently healthy and whole. No more blindness, deformity, or deterioration!

For an interesting explanation of that phenomenon, read 1 Corinthians 15:35-58, which says in part: "There are also heavenly bodies and earthly bodies, but the glory of the heavenly is one, and the glory of the earthly is another. . . . So also is the resurrection of the dead. It is sown a perishable body, it is raised an imperishable body. . . . And just as we have borne the image of the earthly, we shall also bear the image of the heavenly."

This transformation is tied in with the second coming of Christ. The Lord Himself will descend from heaven (1 Thessalonians 4:16-18).

New Testament passages also indicate distinct purposes for Christ's return. In His return Christ will bring to Himself all Christians, living and dead, to be with Him forever. The series of events will also include a judgment in which all believers will be rewarded for their faithfulness (2 Corinthians 5:10).

Judgment will be a prominent part of the series of events after Christ's return. "For we shall *all* stand before the judgment seat of God" (Romans 14:10). You can read about judgment in various New Testament books. A study of those passages shows strongly that the judgment will be fair, and that the Judge will be none other than Jesus Himself. As Paul told some Athenian philosophers who asked him about his teachings, "God is now declaring to men that all everywhere should repent, because He has fixed a day in which He will judge the world in righteousness through a Man whom He has appointed, having furnished proof to all men by raising Him from the dead" (Acts 17:30-31). Paul also wrote: "Each one of us shall give account of himself to God" (Romans 14:12).

When will Christ return? No one knows. Jesus said, "Of that day and hour no one knows, not even the angels of heaven, nor the Son, but the Father alone" (Matthew 24:36). He also said that it will be something like the days of Noah—people will continue eating, drinking, and marrying, until it is too late for them to prepare for escape from the destruction which will befall those who have not believed (Matthew 24:40-42).

Scripture does give us general clues that indicate *about* when Christ may come, however. Among the clues or signs are earthquakes, famines, wars, persecutions, the return of the Jews to the Holy Land, increased missionary activity, departures from the faith, lawlessness, and accumulators of wealth. Also, discerning believers may not be overtaken unexpectedly by Christ's return because they *know* Christ may come at any time (1 Thessalonians 5:1-11).

When He does, our own transformation will be swift and thorough (1 Corinthians 15:51-58).

About that time, the world will go through deep trouble (Mark 13:19-23). The period of the most extreme trouble, which is called the great tribulation, will last seven years (or three and a half years according to some interpreters). That period will occur either just before or just after the first return of Christ.

According to my understanding of the sequence, Jesus will first come to earth *for* His people, before the great tribulation; and then He will come to earth once more *with* His people, after that tribulation, to reign on earth 1000 years before we go on to heaven itself. During that 1000-year period, known as the millennium, His governing headquarters will be in Jerusalem. It will be a time of justice and peace such as the world has never known. This idea of the millennium is based on Revelation 20:1-6.

After that comes the final showdown with Satan, ending with Satan's being thrown into the lake of fire (Revelation 20:7-10). Next comes "the second resurrection"—the resurrection of the wicked—to face God in what is called the great white throne judgment. All whose names are not found in the book of life are then sent to the lake of fire about which Jesus warned so clearly.

Heaven—the everlasting home of the saved—is beyond description in human language. But for hints of its glories, read Revelation 21. The greatest thing about heaven, of course, is God Himself, and the visible presence of Christ. "He shall dwell among them, and they shall be His people, and God Himself shall be among them" (Revelation 21:3). "The city has no need of the sun or of the moon to shine upon it, for the glory of God has illumined it, and its lamp is the Lamb" (21:23).

In heaven, each individual believer's reward will be in proportion to the quality of his works while he was on earth. The judgment of believers, which is completely separate from the great white throne judgment of the wicked, is referred to in 1 Corinthians 3:10-15. Paul makes it clear that our salvation does not depend on our works, but our reward in heaven certainly will: "No man can lay a foundation other than the one which is laid, which is Jesus Christ. Now if any man builds upon the foundation with gold, silver, precious stones, wood, hay, straw, each man's work will become evident; for the day will show it, because it is to be revealed with fire; and the fire itself will test the quality of each man's work. If any man's work which he has built upon it remains, he shall receive a reward. If any man's work is burned up, he shall suffer loss; but he himself shall be saved, yet so as through fire" (3:11-15).

In a long, serious talk with His disciples, Jesus once illustrated the process of judgment graphically. He said that the people of the world would be divided into two groups. He referred to believers as sheep. He referred to unbelievers as goats. Read what He said in Matthew 25:31-46. People who live in Palestine or visit there are familiar with the kind of shepherding Jesus used as an illustration, because even today shepherds keep sheep and goats together, and at certain times they separate the two, just by facing the flock and tapping each animal with a staff, either on the left side of the head or on the right.

What may surprise you about Jesus' application of this illustration is that the basis for this general judgment is works—what good things we do for others. Those who pass have fed the hungry, given drink to the thirsty, invited strangers into their homes, clothed the naked, attended the sick, and visited prisoners. How is it that an eternal destiny is based on works? How does this fit with Ephesians 2:8-9, which says, "By grace you have been saved through faith; and that not of yourselves, it is the gift of God; not as a result of works, that no one should boast"?

The answer is that we are saved by faith and yet as James and other Bible books show, faith that is real shows itself in works. "Faith, if it has not works, is dead, being by itself" (James 2:17). The sheep-and-goats illustration applies to the judgment of faith's expression rather than to faith itself. The result of this general judgment is an eternal division of mankind, one group receiving eternal punishment and the other eternal life (Matthew 25:46).

What does the doctrine of last things mean to you?

God is in charge of your future. If you're one of His by your own choice, Jesus has an indescribably wonderful place in heaven prepared for you. He will come to welcome you to Himself and to that place—a place where love, peace, and joy will completely replace sin, hate, war, fear, pain, and death.

It's really for *you*. You can put your own personal pronoun into each verse of Titus 2:11-14 and read it this way: "The grace of God has appeared, bringing salvation to *me*, instructing *me* to deny ungodliness and worldly desires and to live sensibly, righteously, and godly in this present age, looking for the blessed hope and the appearing of the glory of *my* great God and Saviour, Christ Jesus; who gave Himself for *me*, that He might redeem *me* from every lawless deed and purify for Himself a *person* for His own possession, zealous for good deeds."

Both heaven and hell are real. Both are forever. And after this life there's no second chance. So it's crucial to be ready for Christ's any-moment return. The New Testament repeatedly teaches us to anticipate His coming and to keep our hearts right with Him—encouraging each other, and seeking to win the lost to Christ before it's too late.

People who really believe this doctrine find that it changes every aspect of their lives. Some Christians seem to feel that what's ahead is so remote or so hard to understand that they just won't think much about it now—they'll "just enjoy it whenever it happens." But knowing what God has revealed about your future can make even your here-and-now life more exciting and meaningful. And it prepares you to be of greater service to Christ.

"Now we are children of God, and what we will be has not yet been made known. But we know that when He appears, we shall be like Him, for we shall see Him as He is. Everyone who has this hope in Him purifies himself, just as He is pure" (1 John 3:2-3 NIV). Expecting His appearance helps motivate you to be the kind of person you know He wants you to be.

Neither awareness of Christ's promise nor alertness for His actual return will make you "so heavenly minded that you're no earthly good" if your attitude about it is in keeping with Jesus' purpose in revealing the facts He taught. "Be on the alert," Jesus said, "for you do not know which day your Lord is coming" (Matthew 24:42).

When He comes you'll be transported "in the twinkling of an eye" (1 Corinthians 15:52)—as fast as an angel can travel, faster than the speed of light. One second you'll be here on earth, and the next second you'll be in His presence. It's fairly easy to imagine the excitement of such a gathering from around the world. But far beyond imagination is the deep and lasting thrill of being with Him and with all of the redeemed always.

The Bible tells how the people of God will respond when all get together in the presence of Christ. It says we'll overflow with joy and praise to the Lamb, Jesus Christ, who will then make His declarations as the completely fair Judge, and will reign as the beloved and wise King.

John's advice to Christians in the light of this

impending series of events is: "Abide in Him, so that when He appears, we may have confidence and not shrink away from Him in shame at His coming" (1 John 2:28). This is great advice, because we're watching not just for signs, not just for events, not just for transportation to a *place*, but for the face-to-face appearance of the most wonderful Person who ever lived: Our Lord, our Saviour, our eternal Friend—Jesus Christ.

Not Really Riddles
but you'll have to think!

What do you think were God's reasons for revealing as much as He has about His return, the rapture, the coming judgments, and other future events?

What do you think were His reasons for not revealing more of the future than He has?

Read Mark 13:33-37. What did Jesus mean by *watching*?

What are the big differences between the great white throne judgment and the judgment seat of Christ?

Unbind Your Mind
with these capsule definitions

eschatology—the study of "last things" such as Christ's return, judgment, heaven, and hell

great white throne judgment—the future judgment of the ungodly

hell—the place of the dead, also called Hades

judgment seat of Christ—Christ's future assigning of rewards to each Christian according to his faithfulness

lake of fire—the place of eternal punishment of the wicked, also called Gehenna

millennium—the thousand-year reign of Christ on earth, after His return

prophecy—the foretelling of future events

rapture—Christ's return to earth for His people

resurrection—being made alive again after death

tribulation—deep trouble